## Ann Sandham

Ann has edited *The Women Writers' Handbook* 2020 for Aurora Metro as a guest editor. In her day job, she is a Commissioning Editor for Ladybird Children's Books at Penguin Random House. Previously, she worked at Cambridge University Press commissioning and editing educational textbooks and examinations.

This special 30th anniversary edition was published in the UK in 2020 by Aurora Metro Books 67 Grove Avenue, Twickenham, TW1 4HX www.aurorametro.com info@aurorametro.com

*The Women Writers' Handbook* 2020 copyright © 2020 Aurora Metro Publications Ltd. Cover design copyright © 2020 Aurora Metro Publications Ltd.

Editors: Ann Sandham, Christian Muller and Cheryl Robson

With thanks to: Marina Tuffier, Sumedha Mane, Bella Taylor, Z.A. Raghdo, Ferroccio Viridiani

The copyright in the individual literary and artistic works in this volume remains with the originators of those works, with the exception of any works which are currently designated as being in the public domain.

All the images in this volume are reprinted with permission of the artist, or else they are considered to be Open Source or in the public domain. Every effort has been made to ascertain and acknowledge copyright status, but should there have been any oversight on our part, we will endeavour to fix this. If you believe we have made a mistake, please let us know: editor@aurorametro.com

*Choices: The Writing of Possession* Copyright © A.S. Byatt 1994; *Anne Hathaway* by Carol Ann Duffy. Reproduced with permission of the Licensor through PLSclear; *Early Women Writers* copyright © Philippa Gregory 2020; *The Writing Life* copyright © Jackie Kay 2020; *My Mother Reading a Novel* copyright © 2020, Madeleine Thien; *Interview with Sarah Waters* copyright © Sarah Waters 2020 Artwork p. 32 © 2020 Clare Brienza illustrationsbyclare.com;Artwork p. 97 © 2020 Colleen ODell pixabay.com/fi/users/starglade-768093/;Artwork p. 127 © 2020 Selina Tusitala Marsh tusitala.nz/;Artwork p. 198 © 2020 Susannah Felstead susannah-f.co.uk/ All rights are strictly reserved. For rights enquiries contact the publisher: rights@aurorametro.com

No part of this publication may be reproduced, stored in or introduced into a retrieval system, or transmitted in any form, or by any means (electronic, mechanical, photocopying, recording or otherwise without the prior permission of the publisher. Any person who does any unauthorised act in relation to this publication may be liable to criminal prosecution and civil claims for damages.

This book is sold subject to the condition that it shall not, by way of trade or otherwise, be lent, resold, hired out, or otherwise circulated without the publisher's prior consent in any form other than that in which it is published and without a similar condition being imposed on the subsequent purchaser.

Printed in the UK by 4edge printing, Essex.

ISBNs: (print version) 978-1-912430-33-8 (ebook version) 978-1-912430-34-5

# THE Women WRITERS' HANDBOOK

### 30th Anniversary Edition

### ed. Ann Sandham

AURORA METRO BOOKS

# Contents

| | |
|---|---|
| **Foreword** by Cheryl Robson | 9 |
| **Women's Voices** | |
| - *Choices: The Writing of Possession* by A.S. Byatt | 15 |
| - *Becoming a Writer* by Saskia Calliste | 21 |
| - *Jenny* – a song by April De Angelis | 29 |
| - Interview with Kit de Waal | 33 |
| - *Anne Hathaway* by Carol Ann Duffy | 41 |
| - *Let the World Burn through you* by Sian Evans | 43 |
| - *Early Women Writers* by Philippa Gregory | 50 |
| - *The Creative Process* by Mary Hamer | 55 |
| - *The Writing Life* by Jackie Kay | 60 |
| - *Screen Diversity* by Shuchi Kothari | 63 |
| - *Writing Plays* by Bryony Lavery | 68 |
| - *The Novelist as Wanderer* by Annee Lawrence | 71 |
| - Interview with Roseanne Liang | 77 |
| - *Mei Kwei, I love you* by Suchen Christine Lim | 81 |
| - *The Badminton Court* by Jaki McCarrick | 98 |
| - Interview with Laura Miles | 104 |
| - *The Motherload* by Raman Mundair | 110 |
| - *The Feminist Library* by Magda Oldziejewska | 113 |
| - *Fortune Favours The Brave...* by Kaite O'Reilly | 116 |
| - Interview with Jacqueline Pepall | 120 |
| - *The Art of Translation* by Gabi Reigh | 128 |

- *Conditions of Amefricanity* by Djamila Ribeiro 132
- *Inspiration: Where does it come from?* by Fiona Rintoul 142
- Interview with Jasvinder Sanghera 145
- *A Room of One's Own ...or Not?* by Anne Sebba 152
- *Being a Feminist Writer* by Kalista Sy 156
- *Mslexia* by Debbie Taylor 161
- *My Mother, Reading a Novel* by Madeleine Thien 166
- Interview with Claire Tomalin 175
- *Fortune* by Ida Vitale, transl. Tanya Huntington 181
- Interview with Sarah Waters 183
- *Virginia Woolf...100 years on* by Emma Woolf 189

**Writing Workshops**
- How to run one 200

**Workshop sessions:**
- Self-Assessment 201
- Becoming a Writer 202
- A Room of One's own 204
- Developing Complex Characters 205
- Clichés, Lies and Exaggerations 206
- Mothers/Fathers 208
- Fear of Failure 209
- Self-censorship 211
- Subverting Fairytales 212
- Conflict/Violence 214
- Voice 215
- The Personal and the Political 216
- Resolutions 217

**Resource Directory** compiled by Saskia Calliste 219
**Quiz** 224

*"A woman must have money and a room of her own if she is to write fiction."*
— Virginia Woolf

# FOREWORD

## Cheryl Robson

This book has been published to celebrate Aurora Metro's 30th anniversary as an indie publisher. In compiling this book, we reached out beyond our local network to women writers of all kinds in the UK and beyond. The resulting collection is full of moving and insightful stories, essays, poems and interviews.

In addition, we have included the writing workshops from the original edition of the book and updated the handy resource directory. There is really something for everyone in this volume.

**Indie Publishing**

Little did I know when I began a small literary project in 1989, to publish women's writing gathered from a series of creative writing workshops, that it would lead to the development of an independent publishing company with a diverse list of over 200 authors from around the world.

Motivated by a desire to share the wonderful material collected from the many workshops led by myself and co-tutor Janet Beck at the Drill Hall Arts Centre in Central London, we embarked on the exciting journey to publish a book.

Desktop publishing was in its infancy, and it was this access to new technology, much like the opportunities that digital technology has given to self-publishers today, which allowed us to publish a book by typing all the text on to a floppy disk and passing it to our local printers. Virago was in its heyday, led by fellow Aussie Carmen Callil, and so there was a

## THE WOMEN WRITERS' HANDBOOK

prosperous trail to follow. Carole Spedding at Feminist Book Fortnight and Ros de Lanerolle at the Women's Press offered us some mentoring and once we were apprized of an ISBN number we were all set to go.

The original *Women Writers' Handbook* was launched in 1990, garnering some nice reviews and promoting the work of its many contributors, mainly to friends and family. Women in Publishing were so impressed by our chutzpah in setting up our own small press that they awarded us the Pandora Prize, which came in the form of a beautiful antique writing console, held for a year, before being passed on to the next winner, who happened to be Ros de Lanerolle.

Encouraged by this warm reception, we went on to publish a collection of contemporary plays by women, which won the Raymond Williams Publishing Prize from the Arts Council and led us (naively) to believe that running a small press might actually be a viable option. In the spirit of equality, we opened the press to publishing writing by men too. As one of the draws of publishing is that you hope to have some influence on the wider society and cultural change, our publications included many pioneering books such as *The Arab-Israeli Cookbook* by Robin Soans which was the first book to give cultural equity to Arabs and Jews in one volume (awarded a Special Jury Prize for Peace by Gourmand World Cookbooks) and *Silent Women: Pioneers of Cinema* co-eds Melody Bridges and myself (voted Best Book on Silent Film in 2016).

The ability to collaborate with others is important and from the outset our publishing programme has been both diverse and international. Recently, e-books and social media have helped to grow our network of contributors and customers. However, the experience we have gained of international distribution, cash flow, budgets, rights and permissions has been hard won. Thirty years on, we are thrilled to include the work of so many wonderful authors and illustrators in this handbook, and we hope that this new edition will entertain and even inspire you.

### Feminist ups and downs

There are many feminisms today but the guiding principle is that all human beings have equal rights and opportunities. Acknowledging the debt we owe to early feminists, we have published several suffrage plays in

## FOREWORD

*Votes for Women and other Plays* ed. Susan Croft, and to mark the centenary of women gaining the right to vote, we launched *The Original Suffrage Cookbook*, ed. L.O. Kleber, a revised edition of a 1915 suffrage cookbook originally published in the US. Leading feminist voices from the 60s and 70s are featured in our list too, with Germaine Greer's adaptation of *Lysistrata*, Dacia Maraini's historical play *Veronica Franco, Courtesan and Poet* and Nawal El Saadawi's play *Twelve Women in a Cell*.

In the 90s, we ran the risk of prosecution when we staged readings and published work by LGBT writers, at the time of Thatcher's controversial Clause 28. Under the spurious notion of advancing "quality" in the arts, funding in London for grassroots creatives almost dried up. The debate at the time centred on diversity and intersectionality and we were proud to publish a ground-breaking anthology, titled *Six Plays by Black and Asian Women Writers* ed. Kadija George. The collection included essays by Bernardine Evaristo and Dierdre Osborne among others and plays by Rukhsana Ahmad, Maya Chowdhry, Trish Cooke, Winsome Pinnock, Meera Syal and Zindika.

Despite having a woman prime minister, feminism in the UK suffered a backlash. A new kind of modern woman – the "ladette"– became cool. Later, the Spice Girls were able to re-brand feminism under a girl-power banner and monetize their version of Britpop to a global audience. In the art world too, Tracey Emin challenged traditional ideas with her piece *My Bed* (1998), depicting the detritus of a modern woman's life, while Sarah Lucas satirized patriarchal notions in her witty visual images and sculptures. In the USA, Riot Girrrl and punk subculture led the way, while queer theory and "transfeminism" raised issues around gender identity.

Over the last decade, a new energy has reignited feminist activism, as women have come together on social media and the internet to challenge continuing male bias and discrimination. Since 2018, a group of radical independent bookshops around the UK and Ireland have organized Feminist Book Fortnight to celebrate feminist books for a new readership. Encouragingly, this new feminist activism can be seen happening all around the world, motivating younger women and some men to speak out, reigniting the debate on gender equality. Movements such as #MeToo and

## THE WOMEN WRITERS' HANDBOOK

#TimesUp have helped us tackle the ongoing issues of wage inequality, sexual harrassment at work, body autonomy and rape culture.

Although female authors top the bestsellers' lists there's a lack of diversity and a preponderance of men in top jobs within publishing. Reviewers too, even when female, tend to favourise books by men. To improve the representation of women in the arts and other fields, we have launched a series of books entitled *50 Women in...* to bring attention to the fantastic women working in many fields, who have achieved considerable success, in spite of the remaining obstacles.

**The Virginia Prize for Fiction**

Evaluating the manuscripts that found their way to our submissions pile in 2009, we found that 65% were written by men. To improve this, we launched a new competition for women writers named in honour of local writer Virginia Woolf who lived in Richmond from 1914-1924. With husband Leonard Woolf, the couple established the Hogarth Press, a small publishing venture, in their home. The Virginia Prize for Fiction is now a biennial competition run with the aim of developing and publishing women novelists writing in English. In 2017, we started a campaign to erect a full-sized bronze statue of Virginia Woolf – the first in the UK. The book *Virginia Woolf in Richmond* by Peter Fullagar followed, to give insight into the writer's life in the town. We now offer talks to community groups on the subject. A 20 per cent share of the profits from this book will go to the Virginia Woolf statue project. To find out more or donate, go to: www.aurorametro.org/virginia-woolf-statue

During the making of this book we've been on lockdown due to the Covid 19 virus; normality ruptured. The recognition of our interconnectedness and vulnerability as human beings have given us pause for thought. Our dreams of a more equal world beckon us. Will we fight for systemic change? Will we birth a better future?

**Cheryl Robson** is an award-winning writer, publisher and filmmaker. She was shortlisted for the ITV National Diversity Award for Lifetime Achievement 2019. Her acclaimed documentary *Rock 'n' Roll Island* aired BBC4 (2020) and was named a Sunday Times Critics' Choice programme.

# WOMEN'S VOICES

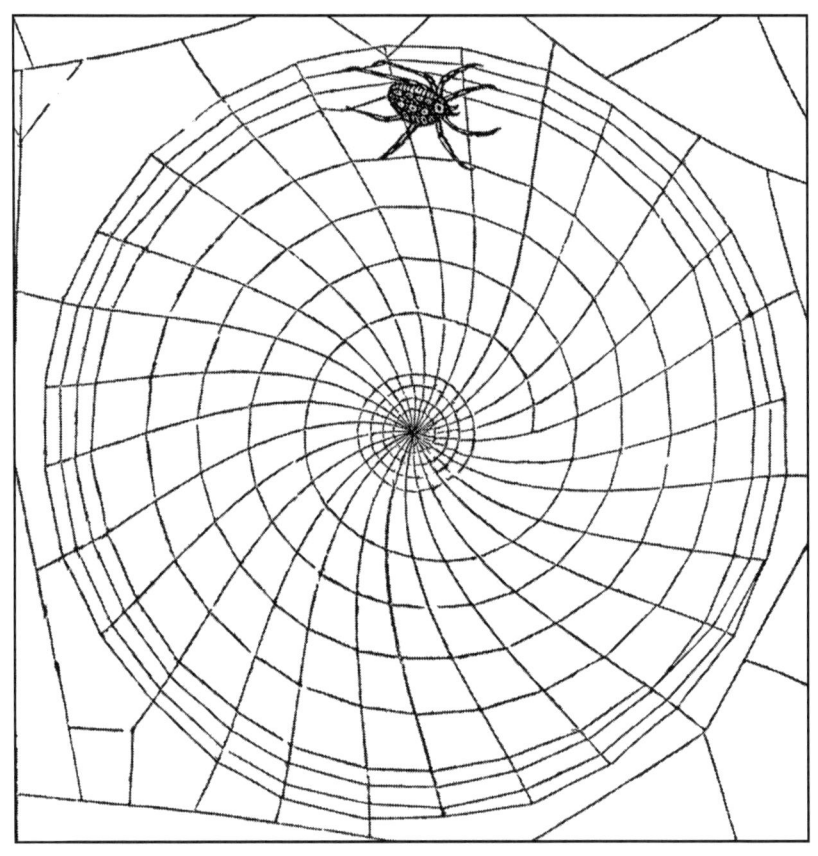

# CHOICES: THE WRITING OF POSSESSION

## A.S. Byatt

The beginning of *Possession*, and the first choice, was most unusually for me, the title. I thought of it in the British Library, watching that great Coleridge scholar, Kathleen Coburn, circumambulating the catalogue. I thought: she has given all her life to *his* thoughts, and then I thought: she has mediated his thoughts to me. And then I thought, "Does he possess her, or does she possess him? There could be a novel called *Possession* about the relations between living and dead minds." This must have been in the late 60s. It was the time of the *nouveau roman*, of the novel as "text".

When I first recognize a thought as the germ of a novel or story, I form a shape, or file, in a corner of my mind, to which I add things that seem to belong to it, quotations, observations. At that stage this *Gestalt* is more like the plan for a painting than a novel. It has colour and texture, though I have to think very hard to call these to mind. The *Urgestalt* of *Possession* was a grey cloudy web, ghostly and spidery, to do with the ghostliness and connectedness of the original idea. I think it was also to do with the *nouveau roman*, which I still visualize in that form. I imagined my text as a web of scholarly quotations and parodies through which the poems and writings of the dead should loom at the reader, to be surmised and guessed at.

The next decisive choices came in the 1980s, when I was teaching Browning and George Eliot, and also lecturing on Henry James and his father, Henry James senior, who had been a leading Swedenborgian. I had

had the idea that the word "possession" involved both the daemonic and the economic – Kathleen Coburn had pulled off a notorious *coup* when she bought the Coleridge notebooks for Toronto. Reading the Browning letters made me see that "possession" had a primary sexual connotation, too. I made a decision: there should be two couples, man and woman, one alive and one dead. The novel would concern the complex relations between these two pairs. My grey cobwebby palimpsest changed colour – it took on a lurid black shot with crimson and scarlet, colours of passion. I was teaching that great novel, *The Bostonians*, with its world of "witches, wizards, mediums, and spirit-rappers and roaring radicals" to a generation of students involved in the politics of gender, who disliked Henry James's tragi-comic treatment of lesbian passion. It occurred to me that in the world of nineteenth-century spiritualism and feminism, possession had both its meanings at once. So there was a need for the nineteenth-century woman to be a lesbian, or thought to be a lesbian, and the twentieth-century woman scholar to be a feminist. What George Eliot's letters added to this texture of texts to think about was the sense I always have that her real passionate self is splendidly absent from the letters kept by the people who kept them. Her love-letters, unlike those of the Brownings, were buried with her. It is the luck of an unusually devoted marriage between poets once separated that we have the Browning letters. There have been serious proposals to dig up George Eliot. There is a Gothic plot, I thought, of violence and skulduggery. The *Gestalt* got more lurid, purple, black, vermilion, with flying white forms.

I half-knew that the form of my novel should be a parody of every possible form, popular and "high culture", when I was asked to review Umberto Eco's *Reflections on the Name of the Rose*. I had already had the idea that *Possession* should be a kind of detective story, with the scholars as the detectives, when I read *The Name of the Rose*, which combines medieval theology, Church history, gleefully bloodthirsty horrors, reflections on the form of the novel, with a hero who is an avatar or precursor of Sherlock Holmes. What entranced me about Eco's *Reflections* was his pleasure – "I wanted to murder a monk", and his technical reflections on the fact that detective stories and melodramas had to be *written backwards*. If you want to burn down a library quickly and irretrievably you must make it

## WOMEN'S VOICES

burnable when you invent its architecture. I had been thinking a lot about the pleasure principle in art. Art does not exist for politics, or for instruction – it exists primarily for pleasure, or it is nothing. It can do the other things if it gives pleasure, as Coleridge knew, and said. And the pleasure of fiction is narrative discovery, as it was easy to say about television serials and detective stories, but not, in those days, about serious novels.

So my novel should be a parody, not of Sherlock Holmes, but of the Margery Allingham detective stories I grew up on. It should learn from my childhood obsession, Georgette Heyer, to be a romance, and it could learn, simultaneously from Hawthorne, Henry James's predecessor, that a historical romance is not realist, and desires to "connect a bygone time with the very present that is flitting away from us". I added things – it should be an epistolary novel, which meant writing the letters the scholars should find; it should contain early narrative forms – Victorian women writers wrote fairy tales – and late ones – bits of biographies and critical "accounts" of what was going on.

The *Gestalt* in my mind changed colour and form and became delicious – all green and gold, the colours of Tennyson illustrations in my mind as a child, of dream landscapes, of childhood imaginings of a world brighter and more jewel-like than this one.

There was a huge problem. I knew that modern forms were parodic – not only Eco, but the intelligent criticism of Malcolm Bradbury had been pointing that out – parodic, not in a sneering or mocking way, but as "rewriting" or "representing" the past. The structural necessity of my new form was that the poems of my two poets, the *most important thing about them* in my own view, should be in this no-longer ghostly text. And I am not a poet, and novelists who write poems usually come to grief. Robertson Davies, the Canadian novelist, had written a novel with a parodic libretto in fact made up of the poems of Thomas Lovell Beddoes. I said to the poet D.J. Enright at a party that I was contemplating using the early poems of Pound that look as though they could be by Browning. "Nonsense," he said. "Write your own."

So I tried. My mind has been full since childhood of the rhythms of Tennyson and Browning, Rossetti and Keats. I read and reread Emily Dickinson, whose harsher and more sceptical voice I found more exciting than Christina Rossetti's meek resignation. I wanted a *fierce* female voice. And I found I was possessed – it was actually quite frightening – the nineteenth-century poems that were not nineteenth-century poems *wrote themselves*, hardly blotted, fitting into the metaphorical structure of my novel, but not mine, as my prose is mine.

There is one further late choice I should like to mention. There are three passages in the nineteenth-century narrative which are recounted by a Victorian "omniscient" third-person narrator. These three include the Epilogue, and tell what might be thought of as the most important, beautiful and terrible moments in the lives of the Victorian characters. I still receive angry letters from time to time from all over the world, saying these passages are a mistake – that I have cleverly told the story of the past through documents, diaries, letters, poems, and am breaking my own convention incompetently. But my decision was very deliberate. It was partly polemical, for two reasons. I do believe that biographies are a kind of shadow-play, and that *what really mattered* is likely to elude the piecers-together of lives. (Doris Lessing endorses this view, mischievously, at the beginning of her recent autobiography.) I also believe that the third-person narrator has been much maligned in the recent past – it does not aspire or pretend to be "God" – simply the *narrative voice*, which knows what it does know. And I wanted to show that such a voice can bring the reader nearer the passions and the thoughts of the characters, without any obligation to admire the cleverness of the novelist. There is a nice irony about this – the writer and reader share what the critics and scholars cannot discover.

And the *Gestalt* now? A green and gold and blue balloon, far away, untouchable. A writer can't think about novels that have gone away. The *Gestalt* of the one I am writing, about the 1960s, is a jagged harlequin pattern of coloured fragments and smoking bonfires. And there is something weak about the narrative line, or tension, connecting these, that I'm trying to deal with.

*This essay was first presented as a speech at Tate Gallery, 12 January 1994 and printed in Threepenny Review, US, July 1995; also in the Independent January 1994.*

# WOMEN'S VOICES

## A.S. Byatt

A.S. Byatt is renowned internationally for her novels and short stories. Her novels include the Booker Prize-winning *Possession*, *The Biographer's Tale* and the quartet, *The Virgin in the Garden*, *Still Life*, *Babel Tower* and *A Whistling Woman*. Her novel, *The Children's Book*, was published in 2009.

Her highly acclaimed collections of short stories include *Sugar and Other Stories*, *The Matisse Stories*, *The Djinn in the Nightingale's Eye*, *Elementals* and *Little Black Book of Stories*. A distinguished critic as well as a writer of fiction, A.S. Byatt was appointed CBE in 1990 and DBE in 1999.

*"I am out with lanterns, looking for myself."*
— Emily Dickinson

# BECOMING A WRITER

## Saskia Calliste

"What do you want to be when you grow up Saskia?" Every few years, my reply would vary drastically, as did the why. "A corporate lawyer because I want a house like the dad from *Clueless*." Growing up black, in and out of council estates, dreaming about more desirable real estate became a form of liberation. I was eight when I coined that particularly bizarre response that would mostly prompt a look of pity which essentially said, "keep dreaming". From everyone except my mum, of course: in the eyes of maternal law, her youngest could do no wrong and would only ever excel in her endeavours: even despite our gipsy-esque lifestyle. By that I mean, ever since I moved to Portsmouth at age five, because of an itch to live by the sea my mum had to scratch, we moved roughly every two years.

I had been to three different primary schools by the time I was eleven. I can't complain too much; the adapt or die instinct is instilled in me, and the older I get, the less I resent, and the more thankful I am for it.

As a child, I spent a lot of time in my head, in the movies I watched and the books I read. I wasn't an introvert, despite the less than friendly neighbourhood racists, whose sole mission was to instill in me that I didn't belong there. I still had friends, and I still played outside: adapt or die. I loved riding my scooter through Bransbury Park come rain or shine. It was in those moments when I had felt the freest. It was a time where I wasn't black in a white town, and I wasn't the fat friend of my more popular peers: I was just a little girl enjoying her freedom.

## THE WOMEN WRITERS' HANDBOOK

When it came to school, I was good at most things, except science. I had always dreamed about going to university as a kid, which is odd because my mum didn't go – she got a job straight out of high school doing secretarial work and followed on that trajectory for much of her adult life. Most of my friends used to dream of just being mums, a concept I've never been able to grasp.

I didn't come to the realization that I wanted to be a writer until I was well on the path to a different career altogether, despite the fact that I had gotten approximately six people into university by writing their personal statements for them. I wanted to study Fashion Communication and Promotion at Central Saint Martins. I was so passionate about it; I would study designers, photographers and stylists in my spare time; I bought *Vogue* monthly, finances permitting; I even created my own fashion line: "Edgy-cated".

As a fat child, I stopped wearing kids' clothes earlier than my peers. I got to shop in the adult section, so I got to experiment more with clothes – that's my optimistic view of the situation anyway. I'd wear things people said fat people shouldn't, but I'd be damned if I was going to be another fat person walking around in black trousers as if that's all there was. "Edgy-cated" was going to be dedicated to fat women everywhere, and I was going to make them shine. I had the ideas, I just needed someone to help me execute them, and where better to find someone than to go to a university dedicated to fashion.

I had tailored all my A' levels to achieving this, and was well into a year's art course, per their request, so that I could study at Central Saint Martins. Art was awful. I've never been able to draw, and I'd never had any desire to learn. I hadn't before been in a position where I was the poster girl for what not to do, yet there I was, surrounded by budding Picassos who could tell I wasn't one of them. I was dangerously close to giving up.

Once, we were making 3D chess pieces based on our country of choice. I chose Japan; my rook was a ninja and my king a samurai. Having made them out of clay, they were left to set in silicone moulds in the drying area. I was slower than everybody and taking longer to clean up, so my lecturer, Paul, decided to help me. "Please don't touch the mould sir, I made the neck too thin, so it's very fragile." Instructions he ignored, and right on cue, the neck snapped against his long, bony fingers. I've always been polite, despite my aversion to male authority, growing up with a single mother, but that day there was no containing it. I yelled, cursed; I thought I was going to combust spontaneously. I threw my sketchbook and the other half of my samurai on the floor in his direction. He jumped back to avoid being hit, looked at me in disgust and said, "Why are you even here?"

The only module I was able to ace was Digital because manipulating images on a computer and creating album covers is something I'm good at. A turning point occurred when some unsung hero added Contextual Studies to my timetable. As they say in poker, "this is where I win my money back." The first essay we had to write was an evaluation of Philippe Starck's "Juicy Salif", the world's most impractical lemon squeezer. The pack of wolves who once laughed at me for not knowing that HB pencils had numbers that actually meant something, had now turned into puppies who needed my help to convey their thoughts.

I had done it: I had come out of the other side with a new goal in life, and that wasn't Central Saint Martins. Surprisingly, it didn't take much for me to let go of the dream I had been coveting for the past three years. I did art because I was told to, I wanted to study fashion because it's something I thought I had to do, but writing came with no such hang-ups. I used to come up with a book idea at least once a day when I was younger. It had always been there; I was just too preoccupied with what wasn't to realize what could be. I left West Thames College at the end of the first year with a "Level Two Subsidiary" art qualification at Merit grade.

B.A. Creative Writing and Journalism at the University of Roehampton is where I landed, followed by an M.A. in Publishing. I knew I'd be surrounded by people who were writing novel extracts before they could walk, and I'd only just decided I wanted to be a writer. To say I was nervous was an understatement, but studying art had prepared me for the worst. I had spent the summer before starting university familiarizing myself with the classics, just in case someone tested me and then made it their mission to expose me as a fraud.

Within the first few weeks, I had hit a bump. There was no such thing as a "lightbulb moment" according to my lecturer Nancy. Well, that's me done then, I thought. All my ideas began as "lightbulb moments" that I fought to channel into existence. I got my ideas mostly when I was doing something menial, riding the bus or cleaning my room. I made the mistake of telling Nancy that once, whose response was less than encouraging: "Well if anyone has any cleaning they need doing, just get Saskia to do it, and she might get a book out of it." I didn't speak out much in her class after that. I already felt I didn't fit into the mould of what a writer should act or think like, and she had confirmed it.

If I learnt anything from my years at Roehampton, it's that people's opinions on writing are completely subjective. Many of the lecturers didn't consider any form of writing that wasn't literary, worth acknowledging. In journalism, however, the writing style was the complete opposite: journalism wanted objective writing that celebrated your tone and personal style.

It took me a long time to be comfortable with my voice, but studying journalism helped me nurture it. It was during my third year, whilst studying Magazine Production and Journalism, when I got a clear idea of the kind of writer I was. Sarcastic in tone, brutally honest in delivery, partial to the odd cliché (careful not to overuse them), with an unexpected hint of optimism.

After university, I ended up writing for *Voice* Magazine UK. The first article I ever wrote was a review of *Hurricane Protest Songs*, a play by the Graeae Theatre Company, and an interview with two cast members. I'll never forget the feeling of walking up to the box office and asking for my press ticket, then being shown to my reserved seat and being told if there was anything else I needed, just to ask.

I had always loved the theatre: I used to act myself. In high school, I was the stage manager for my school's adaptation of Michael Morpurgo's *Warhorse*. In year six, I played Tallulah in our leavers' production of *Bugsy Malone* – I like to say I was the first black Tallulah. Having been to plays for pleasure and work, the absence of cast members who looked like me was more than apparent; but that was nothing new to me, growing up in Portsmouth. For a long time, that's just how I thought the world was. I didn't realize how much of an issue it was until I started to review

## WOMEN'S VOICES

theatre and hear the concerns of the lack of diversity that surrounded the industry.

*Wicked* was the first show I saw in the West End, and it was magical, a far cry from a school production, but the feeling I had was the same. The lack of diversity in *Wicked* is not the first thing that comes to mind when you think of the play, because the message is universal, and I think that's how many West End shows get away with their lack of representation. Theatre is not film, where the scrutiny of it for disproportionately championing the narratives of white people is very public. The root of the problem for film and theatre, however, is essentially the same. The need for diversity and representation in entertainment cannot and will not subside simply by putting BAME actors on stage or in front of the camera. Diversity is needed as much on-screen as it is off-screen; behind the scenes, operating the camera, choreographing the dances and directing the production.

Change has occurred over the past few years with BAME people being appointed as artistic directors for The Young Vic and Bush Theatre, but to say they still have a lot of work to do to counteract years of damage is an understatement. My interest in the theatre comes from my immediate family's love of performing, of books and film – storytelling as a whole – but if I didn't have that, I can't say there is anything out there that would have pointed me in that direction. Writing for *Voice*, I get to see a lot of great underground plays that feature different genders, ethnicities and abilities in an effortless way that mainstream theatre could learn from.

The biggest job I've had working with *Voice* Magazine was covering the Edinburgh Fringe Festival 2019. I saw 35 shows over the course of six or seven days. I lived on tinned pineapple most of the time, barely slept, and wrote drafts of the reviews on the bus back to Musselburgh after a 16-hour day. It was overwhelming, slightly intimidating and wholeheartedly exhausting, but it had this unshakeable energy that ran through the streets.

The first show I reviewed was called *Beach Body Ready*; it was a show about body positivity by a group of women from Hull, The Roaring Girls. They stood on stage, danced, showed their bodies unapologetically and shared some truly heart-breaking stories about their experiences with weight issues. The show was fantastic, and The Roaring Girls had the house in tears. One rule of the Fringe, for *Voice* Magazine anyway, is not to let people know that you're a journalist – a rule I broke. I waited for them after the show because I had to give them my congratulations. There I was, in their dressing room, revelling in their laughter and ecstasy of successfully completing their first Fringe show. It was that moment, seeing them so happy that they had got their first five-star review, that gave me newfound energy for what I was doing.

There was no better moment than seeing reviews that I had written, included on posters promoting shows which I had gone to, just the day before, displayed on the streets of Edinburgh. I was getting retweets and likes from directors and cast members who were so thankful that I understood their vision.

When I was at university, I was tailoring my work to what I thought people wanted to hear as opposed to what I wanted to say. Reviewing was the turning point for me as a writer to know that, good or bad, believe in what you're saying, and people will respond to it.

That simple notion of believing in what you're saying is what's missing from mainstream media. The issue with much current journalism is that trending sells. Hot topics with short shelf lives get more traction than subject areas that affect our society in detrimental ways. Something even worse than that, is when people in the industry with the power to instigate real change, comment on sensitive issues in a controversial manner just to get people talking about them. It gives issues like racism, homophobia and sexism a spotlight, but it's toxic, and it doesn't come from a place of genuine concern or want to do better, but to incite shock and awe.

Giving a voice to those who are rendered voiceless is an important responsibility which journalists, no matter the size of their platform or audience, should do their best to honour. I myself want to tell stories that people can relate to. I like to think I write about pieces of the picture that may seem obscure but make perfect sense when you shed a little light on them. I'm learning every single day, and know I have a long way to go with no idea where I'll end up in the future. If my experience as a writer, as a black girl living in Portsmouth, and as a human being, has taught me anything, it's that the where is not what matters, just as long as you don't lose yourself along the way. And if you do, let's hope you have a mum like mine, locked and loaded with a total cliché that, for some reason, coming from her, is the jolt you needed to remember why you're even here.

**Saskia Calliste**

Saskia Calliste studied B.A.Creative Writing & Journalism and M.A. Publishing at the University of Roehampton. She is part of an ensemble of students who self-published the *Awake, New Writing* anthology at Roehampton and is a theatre and culture reviewer for *Voice* Magazine, UK. She recently completed a media/publicity internship for Barnes Children's Literature Festival and also an editorial internship at Fincham Press.

"*I knew that if it was what
I was supposed to do,
I would find my way.*"

– Jo Harjo

# JENNY

## a song by April De Angelis

Jenny was a woman who liked her coffee cup
To be made of genuine recyclable stuff
Her shoes were vegan
Her meals were too
Jenny was the owner of
a compostable loo

Jenny rode a bike Jenny ditched her car
Jenny used a canvas bag wore a thrift shop bra
Jenny grew organic veg
Cleaned with ecover
Everything sustainable
Even her lover

Jenny wouldn't fly a plane  Jenny took the train
Wouldn't eat red meat  always campaigned
Jenny voted green  wrote to the queen
Renounced consumer goods
Ate aduki beans
But one day Jenny said enough

## THE WOMEN WRITERS' HANDBOOK

I recycle to the very last tin
Fully exploit my brown garden bin
Grow my own potatoes
Banish plastic straws
But  gigatons of carbon still keep me shakin in my drawers
Felt I was staunching a wound with a plaster
Nothing being done to avert disaster

After thirty years of asking nicely for stuff
Jenny got fed up  Jenny'd had enough
Had enough of pleading  for the planet to be saved
Written letters  marched  been so well-behaved
Come on London Met she said I'm throwing in the towel
You'll have to arrest me cos I'm a rebel now

Jenny stood in the cold  rain poured on her head
And when the police said move on dear
Jenny she saw red
I'm here so my kids can live a full life span
So do your worst Mr policeman

Sick of politicians sick of the press
Thumbing their nose at me they don't impress
So when the policeman read her Section 14
Jenny said to move me you're gonna need your team

They put Jenny in a van  took her to Brixton nick
She chose the vegan option  Jenny read a book
When she stood before the judge on her judgement day
Jenny she went to town with what she had to say

## WOMEN'S VOICES

I recycled to the very last tin
Fully exploited my brown garden bin
Grew my own potatoes
Banished plastic straws
But gigatons of carbon kept me shitting my drawers
Felt I was staunching a wound with a plaster
Nothing being done to avert disaster

Jenny said I stood up for the earth I did
Judge agreed with Jenny fined her a hundred quid
Jenny took it on the chin Jenny ate some cake
Made with non-dairy for the planet's sake
Said guess I'm a criminal and all that it took
Was Sir David Attenborough to make me a crook

You can meet Jenny now on your local street
Handing XR leaflets to everyone she meets
Say hello to Jenny she'll say hello too
And if she's feeling in the mood she'll sing this song to you


**April De Angelis**
April De Angelis' plays include: *Jumpy* (Royal Court, West End, Sydney) *Playhouse Creatures* (Old Vic, Chichester) *A Laughing Matter* (NT) *A Warwickshire Testimony* (RSC) *Flight* (Libretto, Glyndebourne, International) *The Village* (Stratford East) *My Brilliant Friend* (Olivier Theatre)

Artwork by Clare Brienza

# INTERVIEW WITH KIT DE WAAL

Q. **How has it felt, the amount of attention you've got since your first novel a few years ago? Did you expect this kind of appetite for your work?**

A. No, no, absolutely not. I'm still very surprised by it. Delighted, obviously. It is very, very surprising to me. I came to publishing and to writing relatively late in life – didn't get published till I was 56. And all I'd heard for 10 years is how hard it was to get published, how hard it was to make your mark, so I'm still very surprised that that hasn't been my experience.

Q. **There are lots of different opinions about doing writing courses. You did the MA writing course at Oxford Brookes. What is your opinion?**

A. I think it's really important to learn the craft of writing, however you learn it. So it's exactly like if you want to go from being a cook, to being a chef: you have to learn the craft. It's very difficult to make that leap from cooking Spaghetti Bolognese at home to making cordon bleu for twenty. In fact, what you're doing when you stop writing for yourself and start writing for publication, is that you're trying to become an expert. So I do believe that courses and training and learning the craft can help. By the same token, there are people that transition from cook to chef, lots and lots of people, through hours and hours of practice. So, no, you don't have to do a £10,000 creative writing masters degree – although they are great, and the majority are very good, very well taught, very well run, and when they're done well I think they're brilliant, absolutely – but that's a stretch for a lot of people to come up with that money, even if it's a student loan, it can still feel very burdensome. So I would say, always, every writer should learn the craft, whether that's by hours and hours of practice on your own, whether it's by taking online courses, going to listen to authors, taking short courses, maybe five courses or six courses, that deal with specific topics like third person or plotting or whatever, or whether you do a masters, but I believe strongly that all writers learn the craft. It just depends on the route you take.

**Q. You've become, perhaps without meaning to, a spokesperson for the working class voice in literature and in art. What aspects of working class life, particularly women's lives, do you think need more attention in the arts and in literature?**

A. The fact that women come to literature and the arts generally later in life ... I don't know many women at all who don't multi-task, that haven't got five or six different hats, whether that's mother, partner, carer, employment, whatever it is, there's so many different things that we do, and writing gets squashed into the margins, to the very edges. And I think what happens is when sometimes there's a taste of freedom in your forties or fifties, women start saying, "Ok, now I could have some time, and do what I want to do," and that could mean being an artist or a writer. And yet the industry really favours the young. It loves nothing better than a début by a 25-year-old woman, or man, or anybody – but a 25-year-old. Lots and lots of prizes, for example, prioritise young people and exclude older people, which has a disproportionate excluding effect on women particularly. Also, of course, there's the perception that women write about light subjects, they write about domestic subjects, or they write genre fiction, like romance. And actually, the serious questions of the day are tackled, and are the exclusive preserve of men. And that's also really, wrong, really an imbalance.

Women do write serious literature, of course they do: there's Margaret Atwood and Toni Morrison, there's hundreds, there's thousands of other examples I could give. So, very much, I think the publishing industry generally, and the arts, not just writing at all, most definitely all the arts, need to think about giving attention to women and to older women in particular.

**Q. You mentioned genre: are you conscious when you're writing of fitting the conventions of a specific genre? How does that affect**

## WOMEN'S VOICES

your writing? Because, for example, in *Becoming Dinah* you have this retelling of *Moby Dick*.

A. *Becoming Dinah* was the first time I've ever been aware of writing for genre. I've never, ever written for genre. I was very surprised that *My Name is Leon* is considered literary fiction. I just wrote the book that I wrote. It's really for the publishing industry to say what genre I write in. It is different for "children and young adults" – I think you do have to have very specific things in mind when you're writing for that. Or if you write particularly for "crime", for example, there needs to be a crime. You know, there are certain ingredients for some kinds of genre fiction that you absolutely need to take notice of. I have never had to do that before I wrote *Becoming Dinah*. And in the next novel I'm about to start, I have no idea what genre it will turn out to be. I'm just really trying to write a good book.

**Q. Could I ask about the decisions you've made in your career as a professional writer? Has there been a particularly good decision you can identify, creative or practical, and is there any decision that you perhaps regret?**

A. I don't actually think I've made any decisions – things just happen to me! – getting Jo Unwin as an agent, because she's brilliant, but that really wasn't my decision. It was her decision, I suppose, to invite me to be one of her clients. And I was absolutely overjoyed. I actually did make a decision: when my book went to auction, I had six people that were interested and I chose Penguin. I think that was a really, really good decision. I've had a really good experience being published by them. They've been very supportive. I like what they stand for, I like what they're trying to do. And as for decisions I regret ... no, I don't think so! I think perhaps I could try to take some time off, that might be a good decision to make in the future. But at the moment: no, everything's very good!

**Q. What do you think about the argument that writers should stick to writing about their own experience or their own cultural background?**

A. I think writers make things up. That's writing fiction, we all make things up. And I don't think there's anything wrong with imagining another life or experience. But I do believe that we have to be aware of sensitivities around certain things, make sure that we do our homework, make sure in certain circumstances that we use a sensitivity reader. I wrote *Becoming Dinah* about a young girl who is struggling with her sexual identity, and I did have a sensitivity reader, and a consultant beforehand. I did research with someone who had had a similar experience, and two people. And I also used a sensitivity reader. Because I think there are certain sensitivities you really want to have respect for. It doesn't mean you shouldn't do them, but it does mean we shouldn't be so arrogant that we think we know everything about a subject, or about a life, or about an experience, just because we fancy "having a go".

**Q. What kind of responses have you had from your readers, and are you surprised at their reactions?**

A. I meet a lot of readers at festivals. They contact me online; Facebook, Twitter, on email, on the website. And I can't think of a bad experience I've had. It's just been overwhelmingly positive. People contact me usually to say one of the books has meant something to them, or with a question about a book.

**Q. What advice would you give to an aspiring writer?**

A. It would be: to read, first of all, to read a lot. It's amazing how many people want to be writers that don't read. It's very much like the chef analogy, it's like saying, "I only eat McDonald's, but I would like to make Crepes Suzette!" You have to know what it tastes like, you have to know the ingredients. So you do need to read, even outside the genre you're going to write. If you're writing exclusively science fiction, there's a lot you can learn from reading the classics, for example. Or vice-versa. So read a lot. Find people who will support you in what you're trying to do, and not undermine you, not think it's a hobby. Find people who realise how serious you are about it, if you are serious about it. Learn the craft, as I said before. You do need to learn the craft. And also, write. I don't mean write every day, because loads of people can't write every day, don't want to write every day, but it's important that there is output. So that if you, for example, see a competition that you could enter, you've got something ready. Or if you find an agent, and the agent says, "Do you

## WOMEN'S VOICES

want to send me 10,000 words of what you've written?" Have 10,000 words ready, don't go away and write 10,000 words when someone asks for it, because they'll have lost interest in you by the time you do that. So have something ready to send people, or to enter into a competition in a magazine. So when the opportunity arises, you're ready to go.

**Q. You talk a lot in *Becoming Dinah* about the idea of "finding your tribe". Where did that idea come from?**

A. I have no idea ... No, I do actually. I do remember seeing something on Twitter, possibly. Where someone was slagging off Twitter and saying people should concentrate more on meeting face to face – get rid of Twitter and Facebook, and just have face to face human interaction. And somebody put as a response to that: that's great, if your tribe lives down the road, that's great. If your friends all think like you, that's great. But what if you're gay, living in the middle-of-nowhere? Or if you're just living in the middle-of-nowhere, cut off from people? Or if you're transsexual, or transgender, or disabled, or some other marginalised group? What if you're a black person living in the middle of the Lake District, and you'd like to talk to other people from your background? It's very easy for people to say, "Have human interaction." But actually, your tribe might be scattered to the four winds. And so Twitter and online relationships on forums are really important for people like that. So when I say "find your tribe" it doesn't necessary mean face to face, it just means be aware that there are people somewhere, probably, that think like you. And if they think like you, they might support you in whatever you're trying to do. So for me, it's a sense of community, wherever that community may be or reside. It might be people you'll never ever meet in your life, but they may think and help you with your endeavours, and just make you feel less alone in your life.

**Q. In your biography, there is a lot of "flash fiction". Can you describe that, for somebody who isn't aware of what "flash fiction" is?**

A. "Flash fiction" is an entire story between 200 and 500 words. Normally, if you talk about flash fiction competitions, it's between 200 and 350 words. It's a complete story with a beginning, a middle and an end, and characters, and every ingredient that a novel has, or a short story has. That is what flash fiction is, so it's a micro-story. It's absolutely wonderful for honing the craft of writing.

**Q. You're also a big fan of audio books. And you've also the ambassador for a charity: can you tell me a bit more about that?**

A. Yes, the charity is called 'Listening Books' and it provides free or very, very low cost audio books – current audio books, so all the ones that are currently on sale – for people who would struggle to read. It's not just for people who struggle to read, but it was set up for people with either sight impairment, or they can't hold a book for whatever reason, or they may have dyslexia, or for lots or reasons, have trouble reading printed matter. But it's also for people who like audio books. Lots of us who, for whatever reason, do lots of travelling. Well, I came to audio books through my son, who has dyslexia. But now I'm a complete devotee. He no longer listens to audio books, and I do. I travel a lot and I'm away from home and I don't want to carry lots of books, so I listen to lots of audio books and they are absolutely brilliant. And there's research recently that demonstrated that the part of the brain that's stimulated by reading is stimulated in exactly the same way, to exactly the same extent, by listening to audio books. So people get very sniffy about audio books and there's a lot of them who say, "You should be reading," people who, to my mind, are quite small-minded. This is an answer to that, to say that, "No, there is no difference, it's just as good." It's like radio and the TV. They're different ways of absorbing information.

**Q. On your Twitter account you mention screenwriting as well. Are you writing anything at the moment for the screen?**

A. Yes, I'm writing a few different things. They are just pre-production, in discussion at the moment. I have written two episodes of something that'll appear on telly next year. It's a completely different discipline. It's great. It's really, really interesting. But again, it's a completely different skill, and a different plot completely. But I love it, it's great.

**Q. What do you enjoy most about being a writer, and are there any aspects you don't enjoy so much?**

# WOMEN'S VOICES

A. I love making things up, and I love crafting a sentence, I like working on writing. There are lots of aspects to writing, but the first one's the creating, and the second one is the crafting or editing, making something better. I love both of them. I like being in my own head a lot. Anything I don't like? The amount of time it takes to get something right. It can take a long, long time, although I wouldn't say I don't like it, but I can find that frustrating sometimes.

Q. **Has it been quite a change in your daily life and your routine, to go from your previous professions into being a full-time writer?**

A. It is a change and it's a solitary thing. I like company and I like people. So I suppose it is a difficult aspect to being a writer: it is the isolation, which you absolutely need. But sometimes it would be nice, and sometimes it is nice, to write next to somebody, or to have somebody in the next room to say, "Right, we're going to have a coffee break in half an hour." That's always a nice thing to do.

### Kit de Waal

Kit de Waal was born in Birmingham to an Irish mother, who was a childminder and foster carer and a Caribbean father. She worked for 15 years in criminal and family law, was a magistrate for several years and sits on adoption panels. She used to advise Social Services on the care of foster children, and has written training manuals on adoption, foster care and judgecraft for members of the judiciary.

She was named Future Book Person of the Year in 2020. Her writing has received numerous awards including the Bridport Flash Fiction Prize 2014 and 2015 and the SI Leeds Literary Reader's Choice Prize 2014 and the Kerry Group Irish Novel of the Year.

*My Name Is Leon*, her first novel, was published in 2016 and shortlisted for the Costa Book Award. She has two children and lives in the West Midlands.

*"The worst enemy to creativity is self-doubt."*
— Sylvia Plath

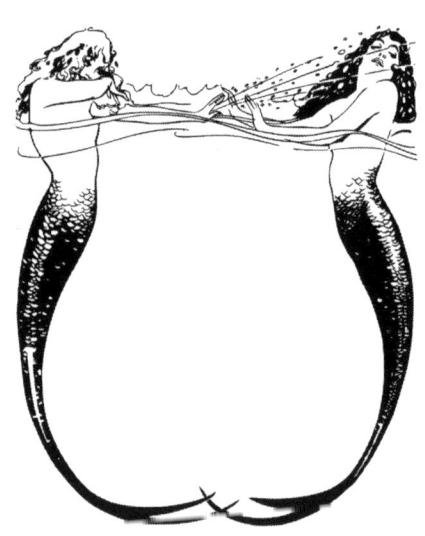

# ANNE HATHAWAY

## Carol Ann Duffy

*'Item I gyve unto my wief my second best bed...'*
(from Shakespeare's will)

The bed we loved in was a spinning world
of forests, castles, torchlight, cliff-tops, seas
where he would dive for pearls. My lover's words
were shooting stars which fell to earth as kisses
on these lips; my body now a softer rhyme
to his, now echo, assonance; his touch
a verb dancing in the centre of a noun.
Some nights I dreamed he'd written me, the bed
a page beneath his writer's hands. Romance
and drama played by touch, by scent, by taste.
In the other bed, the best, our guests dozed on,
dribbling their prose. My living laughing love –
I hold him in the casket of my widow's head
as he held me upon that next best bed.

**Carol Ann Duffy**

Dame Carol Ann Duffy is a British poet and playwright. Duffy first had her poetry published in magazines as a 14-year-old. She went to Liverpool University, graduating with a degree in philosophy in 1977. She worked as a poetry critic for *The Guardian* and as an editor for the poetry magazine *Ambit*. In 1996 she took a post lecturing in poetry at Manchester Metropolitan University, where she later became creative director of the Writing School.

She was the first woman Poet Laureate of Great Britain, serving from 2009-2019.

# LET THE WORLD BURN THROUGH YOU

## Sian Evans

The day my mother found out that I was no longer a virgin – we were standing at the roadside in the middle of town – she pushed me into the path of a car. I wasn't hurt and I don't think she intended to hurt me, she was just enraged. Now 'no nice man' would want to marry me – I was 20 and damaged goods. What would become of me? How would I ever 'do well'?

Doing well meant marrying well. 'Maggie's daughter has done well. She's married a doctor.' This didn't mean that I shouldn't have an education. Nothing was more important to her – having been pulled kicking and screaming out of school herself at the age of 14, she was going to have that opportunity vicariously. I was going to university for her.

This didn't mean that I was exempt from learning how to clean, of course. This was the knowledge that she could pass on – my cultural capital. In the imagined future she had planned for me I would be educated, I would marry well and my 'nice' middle class husband and I would have a lovely home. Would I work? What would I do? Would I have children and if so, who would look after them if I was working? She didn't believe in working mothers. Most importantly my home would be 'spotless'. My mother had a word for women who didn't look after their husbands and homes – not necessarily in that order – they were dedoreth. I'm not sure of its exact derivation. In that part of Wales, many Welsh

## THE WOMEN WRITERS' HANDBOOK

words spawned English approximations, mutating over time until the link between the two was lost. Dedoreth was used, by my mother, exclusively of women. "Look," she'd say, pointing to some hapless man in the bus queue who was well within earshot, "look at the state of that shirt – never been near an iron – Tch, I know his wife, she always was dedoreth." Put simply, it means lazy or stupid or both.

So, she taught me how to iron at seven years old. I enjoyed doing my own handkerchiefs, folding them into ever decreasing triangles. There was something satisfying about smoothing out the creases and making sure that the embroidered initial ended up on top. I wasn't so thrilled when one of my dad's shirts was pulled out of the basket. She had a system – start with the yoke, then continue down to the back, followed by the sleeves and finally the front and collar. Gradually she passed on all her accumulated and mostly self-taught skills. By ten, I knew how to bake fruitcake, how to choose a joint of meat, the right way to clean new potatoes or slice runner beans, how to wash floors thoroughly, how to clean a drain and how to change a plug – I suppose in case there wasn't a man around when your hoover died on you. She had a special kind of contempt for women, like my first sister-in-law, who worked full-time and hired a cleaner. The home came first.

Once I was at university, she was gripped with fear – I was out of range. Only a handful of my peers at school had got places at what we now call Russell Group universities. The struggle to study in a tiny council house with no quiet space other than the garden shed should have convinced her that I was a serious student. But it didn't. My dropping out of university haunted her until the day I shook hands with Princess Anne in the Royal Albert Hall.

We had no phone when I was growing up. I could speak to my friends when I saw them at school – why should I want to contact them out of school? Now, suddenly, they had a phone installed. My hall of residence had one phone to serve a very long corridor. If I was hard to reach then it was my duty to ring home as often as possible. It was a recipe for disappointment.

## WOMEN'S VOICES

Having decided to study French rather than medicine or law, I was already a disappointment. My mother's idea of university was being paid to sit around all day and read books. To be fair, I did have a grant and I did read a lot of books, so she wasn't far wrong. But when, in my second year, I popped home for a few days, suffering, I now realise, from depression, the fear of my quitting returned. I was told to go back – I was "wasting taxpayers' money".

Strangely, once I'd graduated, the pressure stopped altogether. She had no more of a route map for the future than I did. Teaching was mentioned but she was dismissive. She had little time for teachers, a contempt, I think, that sprang from the fact that it was secretly what she'd always wanted to do. But this lack of interference was strangely freeing. I'd long decided that I would not be moving back into the family home and I camped out on a friend's floor in London. 'Signing on' meant I wouldn't starve. My mother seemed to understand my need to be in the capital. My father, however, was baffled. Most of the young women locally, only left home when they married, and they settled a few streets away from their parents.

There were moments when I considered moving back to Wales. I tried to keep abreast of what was going on there. I went to festivals of new writing at the Sherman Theatre in Cardiff. When they tabled an event on women playwrights, I booked in. Arriving late, I crept silently into the dark 400-seater auditorium as the wonderful Elaine Morgan was ushered onto the stage. As soon as my eyes adjusted to the dark I looked around. I was in an audience of one. Why was there so little interest? Not just from the punters but from professionals, men and women working in the theatre, academics, actors? Was it that niche a subject? Where were the other women like me?

When my first play went on in a pub theatre in Camden, I invited my parents. It was their first visit in the five years I'd been living in London. I'm not sure what they expected but it was a tiny venue and a profit-share production. I remember looking over and seeing my dad's eyes fill up at the end. For a man of very few words this spoke volumes. And even when the productions were glossier and the venues much bigger I don't think he was ever prouder.

But it was hard for them to quantify what status meant in this foreign world. I wasn't making much money and it was years before my mother stopped suggesting that I should be a teacher instead. I wasn't interested in teaching and her low opinion of teachers meant her suggestions carried the subtext "why don't you just give up?" When I had my first book published, a translation of the memoirs of an incredibly successful 18th century woman painter – Elisabeth Vigée Lebrun, they didn't come to the launch. There wasn't much of an explanation except that my mother wasn't feeling up to it. When I next saw them, they recounted how a man from an adjoining, and much posher street, whose son I knew at school, had somehow found out about the book. He'd turned up on their doorstep clutching a copy: how proud they must be of me. They were astonished and delighted. His enthusiasm made them rethink – maybe there was some kudos in what I was doing? They followed my work a little more closely from that point on, though my mother's attitude was always ambivalent. On one occasion, she rang to tell me she'd heard a very bad radio review of a play of mine. She was trying to remember the exact wording when I interrupted. I told her it wasn't 'the done thing' to tell someone they'd had a bad review. I later found out that it wasn't even my play that had been slated. My first television play was greeted not with a well done – or we thought it was well written – or we enjoyed it, but a criticism of the production: "Never let that person direct anything of yours again!" When I started writing continuing drama for the BBC my mother was dismissive – "I never watch that kind of thing."

Yet after she died, and I had to clear out the house, I came across a large scrapbook full of newspaper cuttings – reviews and interviews I'd given – things I'd sent her and assumed she'd chucked. I never understood why she (and my father) found it so hard to express their pride to me in person. She was proud but envious too. She loved reading, especially poetry, and in her small Catholic school in Merthyr had taken part in productions of Shakespeare. She had played Portia in one and fifty years later could still recite her speeches. She didn't have the confidence – or the money – to become a mature student. To her, the opportunity to study, to write, to be independent, made me the luckiest person in the world. Why did I need her approval on top of all that?

## WOMEN'S VOICES

But approval is important. The very first piece I wrote was a radio play about two working class girls growing up in Wales before the war. It was rough but it had a public reading. The writers' group I'd joined, made up of mostly older men, damned it with faint praise. I listened politely but later one of the actresses leaned over and whispered to me 'patronising gits'.

I went to see lots of theatre in those early days but it wasn't until I saw a wonderful production by the Women's Theatre Group, that I began to take my future as a writer seriously. Here was a company of women, actors, directors and writers. It was a galvanising moment. As they say, "if you can see it you can be it." That was how I came to write my first full-length stage play, and I felt how I imagine an otter feels, diving into a river for the first time.

There is something intoxicating about hearing actors speak or in recent years, sing, your words and inhabit your creations. More importantly, I still get a huge kick out of watching the audience's reaction. Hearing people laugh (or sob in some cases) is an amazing feeling – far more exciting than applause. You've laid your soul bare, carved it up and distributed it among your various characters. By engaging with the play, the audience shows that they understand. Your desires, your fears, are no longer just yours, they are fears and desires that we have in common.

So, the cultural capital I hand on to my children is quite different. They've been involved in this world from birth. Actors tip-toed around my three-month-old son as he slept on the rehearsal room floor in Theatr Clwyd. My daughter sat in the director's chair while a series I wrote for ITV was being filmed. They come to every show and if I ask, they give me insightful feedback on what I write. They are as proud of their mum as I am of them – which is a lot – and I make sure I tell them as often as I can.

When I broached the subject of having children, my mother batted it away: "Plenty of time." I knew it was because she didn't want to be a grandmother. She was fearful of growing old, of losing her child to motherhood. She also saw children as the end of freedom. Once you had a child, how could you find time to do anything else? This was her experience. Children interfered with her punishing cleaning regime. It was a compulsion, and a futile one at that, and she knew this, but it was also where she found her self-respect and validation.

## THE WOMEN WRITERS' HANDBOOK

I went ahead anyway, mindful of the Cyril Connolly line, "There is no more sombre enemy of good art than the pram in the hall" oft-quoted by a former boyfriend. Before the kids, I would angst over every line, rewriting way past the point when it served a purpose. But now that I physically couldn't keep rewriting, now that I had to hand it in as it was, I felt liberated. Being with children made me less neurotic, not more. As writers, we can spend a lot of time in our heads and this can be a pretty stuffy and airless place. The children dragged me out into the fresh air. They were vital and loving and funny, as well as exhausting and frustrating, but above all, they were real.

Despite her initial fears, my mother faced the real too. She loved her grandchildren to bits but her critical roving eye was never still. Had I ironed the children's vests? No. Had I made that pastry myself? No. When was the last time I cleaned behind the sofa? I can't remember. Like most people I internalised the parental voice and from time to time, when retrieving a long-lost pair of glasses or a half-eaten piece of fruit from the back of said sofa, I still imagine her disapproval. But I tell my children to choose chaos and life over perfection, that childcare and housework are responsibilities to be shared. Most importantly, for my daughter, getting on with life and embracing imperfection will not make her dedoreth. Later in life, Cyril Connolly seemed to have a change of heart too. In *The Unquiet Grave* he wrote "Approaching forty, sense of total failure: Never will I make that extra effort to live according to reality which alone makes good writing possible."

The subjects we write about change as we get older. I've never exclusively written about working class women, but they continue to be at the heart of what I write. I know that my mother didn't see her life as a worthy subject. She scoffed when people said they were proud to be working class: "what is there to be proud of?" She'd internalised the snobbery and hardship and her suppressed rage eventually calcified into a harsh and judgemental personality. It took me a long time to realise that I wasn't a writer despite my background, but because of it. Because I had two vantage points, I could inhabit two spaces and understand both. Emotionally, it's a place of vulnerability and privilege. So now I am more determined than ever to write about women like her with

## WOMEN'S VOICES

their aspirations, their love of poetry, their humour and their kindness, their insight, and their anger. We may be moulded by our circumstances, but we should not be defined by them.

### Sian Evans

Born and brought up in Bridgend, Wales, Sian Evans studied French at Royal Holloway, University of London. She began her writing career as a translator before moving into writing and translating plays. She has written for the National Theatre, Sheffield Crucible, Liverpool Playhouse, Riverside Studios, Theatre Clywd and The Arcola among others. Her stage play *Terra* was shortlisted in Amnesty International's *Protecting The Human* competition. She has also written extensively for radio and TV and has created series for ITV and RTE.

In 2015 she wrote her first libretto, *Hirda*, for the opera company NOISE. A second libretto *Navigate the Blood* was nominated for a Herald Scottish Culture Award in 2019. She is now working on her third libretto with composer Gareth Williams. She is also a Lecturer in Scriptwriting at the University of East Anglia.

# EARLY WOMEN WRITERS

## Philippa Gregory

The first named woman published in the English language may be Hugeburc, an English nun of the 8th century who wrote a biography of St Willibald and St Winnebald. It was not till modern historians translated this manuscript that they found the simple but history-making claim:
*I, a Saxon nun named Hugeburc, wrote this.*

Later women authors were also women of the church, or mystics like Julian of Norwich or Margery Kempe. Julian may have written her own words, but Margery Kempe's account was written by a clerk and published by a later editor. Some women published as translators – Thomas More's daughter Margaret Roper published a translation of the theology of Erasmus in 1522.

The first original woman author, writing in English and putting her name on the text was – of all people – the last wife of Henry VIII, Kateryn Parr. Ignored by history as the "last" wife, the "nurse of Henry's old age", this extraordinary woman theologian and scholar published *Lamentations of a Sinner*, in 1546 or 1547 (after her murderous husband's death). She had previously published anonymously a translation of *Psalms and Prayers* in 1544 and *Prayers and Meditations* in 1545.

Kateryn Parr (as she signed herself) was the first woman to publish under her own name in the English language and women who published after her also tended to write of their spiritual journeys or compose devotional books. The subject of spirituality was seen as the only excuse for the immodesty of publication by a woman, until the anarchy of

## WOMEN'S VOICES

the Civil War years meant that women writers felt able to challenge the tradition of anonymity or silence.

*"Why should not (women) write, I pray? Have they not souls as well as men...?"*
— Sarah Jinner, 1658

The exiling of family members, the disruption of family life during the Civil War meant that women wrote personal and emotional letters to their families and loved ones. Bonds could only be maintained by writing, advice and instruction given in writing to children, warnings and news to members of the family. Even though most of these letters were private, and remained unpublished, they developed a tradition of writing among women, and this tradition was emotional and personal. Women also wrote scientific texts, herbals and receipt books. Sarah Jinner (quoted above) published almanacs.

Women poets felt emboldened to publish, and with the Restoration and the coming of women actors to the stage, women writers (most famously Aphra Behn, but there were others), published plays as well as novels and poetry under their own names. The wildly eccentric Margaret Lucas Cavendish (1623–73) published her thoughts on science, theology and poetry.

In the 1700s, the war of words about the nature of women, in misogynistic pamphlets, led women to enter journalism and write essays to defend their sex. But even then they acknowledged the tradition that an idealized woman should be silent and modest — usually explaining that they had been driven into print to defend themselves.

As ideas grew more liberal and the century wore on, women authors started to explore the histories of women, and were inspired to write descriptions of women in biographies, in fictionalized biographies and in full-on fiction in the new "novel" form. Mary Hays, friend of Mary Wollstonecraft the early feminist, produced a massive six-volume history: *Female Biography, of Memoirs of Illustrious and Celebrated Women of all Ages and Countries*, in 1803. She also wrote essays, journalism and novels. Hays, Wollstonecraft and hundreds of other women became professional writers, making a living from publishing their writing. Mary Wollstonecraft used the novel form to argue for equality for women.

Taking advantage of the "explosion" of novels from the new mass-market printing presses, and the evolution of the new novel form, women writers created the modern novel, publishing often anonymously (like the Brontës) and writing in secret (like Jane Austen), working as if it were a shameful secret, while creating one of the greatest literary forms. Indeed, Tobias Smollett, the successful professional novelist, complained that the anonymous woman authors were producing so many novels that they were driving down the price for "real" writers like himself.

The Victorian novel was largely written by women authors, and it was women like George Eliot in 1871 who (publishing under a man's name to avoid criticisms of indelicacy) made the triumphant merging of the intensely personal story with the sweep of history. *Middlemarch* is a deeply serious work which shows the power of the novel form to describe many lives, many events, and also their meaning; not just in the provincial town of the novel but in the greater moral universe.

And then – surprisingly – there is a collapse of women novelists. The Universities of Illinois and California used an algorithm to examine 104,000 works of fiction dating from 1780 to 2007, drawn mostly from HathiTrust Digital Library and found that women authors wrote half the novels in 1850 – but only a quarter of the novels in 1950.[1] The great novelists of the 20th century, Harper Lee, Maya Angelou, Virginia Woolf, were in a minority.

Why women's contribution to the novel should have declined is not clear from the study. Literary criticism, in the hands of university-educated men at a time when women were not admitted to university, theorized about the novel form, and praised male writers. The increased royalties for successful writers and the status of being a professional writer made the job attractive to male talent, which crowded the market place. Some women writers may have moved to other storytelling mediums. Children's literature has always been a respectable place for a woman author to work. The post-war conventions dictated that married women should be in the house, home-making and cooking, not writing on the kitchen table.

Those women who did publish fiction wrote equally of men and women, and wrote, sometimes with blistering honesty, about the intimate lives of their characters and about their own personal experiences,

---

1 https://www.theguardian.com/books/2018/feb/19/women-better-represented-in-victorian-novels-than-modern-finds-study

## WOMEN'S VOICES

whereas male writers, then and now, tend to write mostly about men, and neglect the female experience.

By the 1960s – when the trend was reversing and women writers were returning to the publishers' lists – a so-called woman's book was no longer a romantic tale about superior male condescending to vulnerable woman (the staple story of the commercial popular novel), but an exploration of female power and female sexuality, such as the novels of Iris Murdoch, Margaret Drabble, A.S. Byatt and Elizabeth Taylor. The feminist movement of 1960s and onward was explored and illustrated in the women's novels of the time.

Today, the explosion of self-publishing means every writer can "publish", even if they do not command a large readership. The online publishing platform FicShelf suggests that 67% of top-ranking titles are written by women. In fiction, the dominance of women authors is even greater – 81% are by women.

What does this tell us? That women have their own views and their own literary style. If prevented from writing they will write in secret, or dictate their stories to male clerks. They will be discouraged by a culture that says that women should not write, they will be discouraged by a culture that says that women cannot write. But if women are allowed to write and publish, they will do so eagerly, expressing themselves at the highest levels of style. And – perhaps, for these are early days – when women are allowed to publish freely they may prove to be more successful than male writers.

### Philippa Gregory

A historian and writer, she has written many novels based on the Tudor period, notably *The Other Boleyn Girl*, which was made into a major film and *The White Queen* which has been dramatised for TV by the BBC.

She founded the charity 'Gardens for The Gambia', which sinks wells to enable market gardening in Gambian schools. She is also a patron of the UK Chagos Support Association, which supports the Chagos islanders in their struggle against the British injustice of being displaced from their homes in the 1960s and 70s for the building of an American airbase.

*"You can't use up creativity.  
The more you use,  
the more you have."*  
    —Maya Angelou

# THE CREATIVE PROCESS

## Mary Hamer

I found myself alone and in prison. Locked up, I didn't even know where. Outside there were sounds of movement and I could hear voices. I wanted people to know that I was there. Desperate as I was to be heard, I halted, paralysed, on the point of calling out: 'But in what language?' I was crying as I woke up.

For myself, the creative process has been a sort of waking up to the world. A quite painful awakening that has extended over a lifetime, though it's not something I used to understand. The world I found myself in on waking was very different from the one I'd been taught to see. The voice I'd been using, the language I'd learned, hadn't truly been mine. I was slow, probably reluctant, to register that dissonance. It took me time to find the urge to describe the world for myself, in a voice that was honest, one that others might hear. This is the story.

When I had that dream in my late twenties, I was an academic. I'd already been published and had no suspicion that the voice I used mouthed a language that was borrowed. I had no idea how that was getting in the way. The very conception of 'voice' as a value was foreign to me. Years passed before I learned about the work of voice coaches in training actors: how many people arrive with their voices more or less 'locked up' and needing to be 'released'. Until that happens they can speak all they like but they won't succeed in being heard.

Today, I have a pretty clear idea of the part that was played by my education in stifling my voice. Not, of course, without my own co-operation.

## THE WOMEN WRITERS' HANDBOOK

Other girls in my class at the convent school took the lessons in doctrine more lightly. For me, though, trained by means of questions to which there were correct answers, the years of catechism were deadening. Taught the supreme importance of 'the universal truths of faith', I learned to sideline my own direct experience of the world. I gave up on what I could see for myself. And with that I also put aside my ability to voice that experience. I had no idea that I was shutting myself down.

The need to fit in at Oxford, the university I moved on to, overwhelmed any nascent impulse of self-discovery. At the time, it also seemed a good idea to lose the trace of Birmingham in my accent. I don't wonder that I wasn't happy during those years. But even though I disappointed my tutors and didn't get a good degree, a drive towards knowing for myself and voicing what I knew was already making itself felt. Something in me sensed that I needed to reconnect voice with experience. Don't laugh: I set out to do a PhD. In those days it meant freedom: you could get away without much supervision. I had taken out a licence to think for myself. And though I never thought of it that way, I was apprenticing myself to a storyteller.

Nowadays, whatever I'm writing about, I try to find the voice of the storyteller. Back then, too inexperienced, too anxious, to create an independent work of imagination, I set myself, instead, to observing how Trollope did it. When it turned out he'd left notes of his daily output, actual columns of figures in little 'working diaries' as he named them, those handwritten figures felt like the first hard evidence on which to base assertions of my own. For a start, I could detect where he had got stuck.

My curiosity, sent to sleep by education, had woken up again. Over time, little by little, instead of responding to some catechism, I found I had questions of my own. Questions about the world I lived in and the way women's lives were ordered. As a girl, it had irritated me to find Shakespeare's Rosalind held up as an ideal of charm. Now that led me to wonder about his other heroines and how they'd been interpreted. I discovered the endless images of Cleopatra, that have been made over the centuries in Europe, while women have been excluded from power and condemned for their sexuality. Working on that book left me more of a woman and less of a disembodied intelligence. It gave me a standpoint.

## WOMEN'S VOICES

With more faith in myself, I went back to school. That is, I enrolled on a month-long intensive theatre training course with Shakespeare & Company in Massachusetts, impelled by an instinct that these people had something vital to teach. There I learned what a difference it could make to be fully in my body and 'on' my voice. When I was invited to write about Shakespeare's play of Julius Caesar, it took me out of the study and away from fixed works of art.

Now, what I wrote was prompted by looking and listening, taking full account of what I could see in the stage picture and what notes of truth or falsehood I picked up in characters' speech. Though I didn't think of it in that way at the time, in learning to pay attention to the language of theatre, I was learning to pay critical attention to the human world around me, the one in which I myself was living. I was being brought fully into the present moment.

However, when I was commissioned to write a book about incest, I came up short against the veto on thinking which shrouds the subject. I was paralysed when I tried to argue: my voice fell back on repeating platitudes. At first, I didn't see how this resembled the state my education had left me in. I couldn't arrive at making sense of my research, the various testimonies I had in front of me. At last, I turned to the voice of the storyteller. Only then did an argument free itself.

Borrowing the stories of abuse told by others, juxtaposing therapists' voices with the stories told by novelists and filmmakers, I found that these built an argument by themselves. They reflected a world in which abuse was widespread and took many forms, not all of them always recognised as such. They linked the damage caused by sexual abuse, the loss of voice and of self-belief, the confusion, with the damage caused by a certain kind of teaching: the sort that in place of encouraging children to explore the world, shrouds it from them in pious mysteries.

If I could now name my catechism days as not merely boring but damaging, the testimonies I'd drawn on had taught me to understand something of greater importance: that the misuse of superior authority in close relationships is not incidental. It is closely connected with the order of power in a world that separates women from men. Far from being an aberration, as I'd always assumed, I could now see abuse as a direct product of the way our human world is ordered. I'd been far too slow to question authority.

This clearing of vision was a breakout moment: I followed it by making a choice that was overdue. As a graduate student I'd wanted to write about Kipling but had been put off by my supervisors. Now I found a renewed interest in him as a survivor. At five years old, Rudyard and his even younger sister, Trix, had been left behind by their parents for years in the power of a foster-mother whose behavior was profoundly disturbing: she tried to break the boy's spirit, while the little girl was exposed to her greedy demands for love.

If this caused them damage, as seemed likely, I asked myself whether that damage could be seen to play out in their later lives, as my previous book had been arguing. But I had lost interest in 'proving' a case through abstract argument. I didn't know if I could do it but I decided my findings would be presented in the form of a novel. But only once I'd worked through the archives and had followed their lives through in detail. I was not interested in making things up. I wanted to test my ideas against the facts. Today, when I'm asked how much of my novel, *Kipling & Trix* is true, I reply, "95%. All I did was join up the dots."

I'd been nervous about trying to write up what I knew in the form of a story. Yet I must have been listening all my life to the voices round me, for creating the necessary dialogue came easily. As it turned out, I'd been a storyteller in hiding all along and fiction was my native language.

**Mary Hamer**

*Kipling & Trix* was awarded the Virginia Prize for Fiction in 2011. Mary's non-fiction books include: *Writing by Numbers, Signs of Cleopatra, Incest: a new perspective* and *Shakespeare's Julius Caesar*.

Mary travels widely and has lectured in many countries. Her work has appeared in the *Economist*, the *Guardian* and the *Independent*. She has contributed to television and radio programmes, such as 'In Search of Cleopatra', 'Women's Hour' and 'Night Waves'. Mary taught at the University of Cambridge for many years and is vice-chair of the Kipling Society UK.

> "The creative adult is the child who survived."
> – Ursula Leguin

# THE WRITING LIFE

## Jackie Kay

The writing life is not an easy life. The writer's life attracts the paradox and the contradiction. It leans towards extremes. We need to be extremely good at being alone to write in the first place, but then we must be good in company too – not just the ordinary company of a few pals round to dinner, but the mega-company of hundreds of strangers and familiars at book festivals and conferences and gigs (as we poets love to call them) the world over. We need self-confidence, but then we need self-doubt in equal measure. We need to be fully tuned into the world, but then we need the ability to switch off from it. We need empathy but then we also need to be self-focused in order to finish our precious books. We need to have a good ear, and a good eye, to be able to listen to the voices of our characters, the tone and the register of our poems. And we need to have the ability to tap in instinctively to the inner voice. We need to be rational, and we need to be open to mystery. We need to tap into the conscious and the unconscious mind. We need to be pragmatic and spontaneous. We need to keep the heart and the door open. But then we need to know when to gently close the door.

It's hard to think of another profession where you can actually do something, but frequently tell yourself that you can't; where the writing of one thing, doesn't help the writing of another. When you can ride a bike or swim, you are pretty confident that when you get back on the bike or in the pool, you'll be able to do it. I imagine when you perform open

## WOMEN'S VOICES

heart surgery that you are pretty confident that you'll still be able to do it, and that the last time will have taught you something. But when you write, you don't begin a poem knowing you'll be able to complete it, or that it will be any good. Your previous experience doesn't count for nothing but doesn't count for something either. When you're in front of the blank page or the screen, you might as well be a virgin. Each new thing is a new beginning, and you are like a young love to the work, shy and uncertain of what you might manage to pull off, what you can get away with.

A writer is never really going to be all that confident about their work, unless they are a raging egoist or a bad writer. And there's the rub. As soon as any pressure is put onto the wound, the blood stops, which is good for the wound but not for the writer's wound. If you put a footballer in a situation of high pressure, a world cup, a Championship final, she or he might suddenly not get that penalty. Writing is as much a game of psychology as football or tennis or golf. But the writer's pressure doesn't come from the open pitch; it comes from within. It comes from the nagging voice that asks: is this really any good? Or from the voice that calls a halt on the muse altogether.

The true writer's most deadly opponent is the writer's own self. Writers get writers' block, the most common ailment and sickness for the writer, a terrifying thing when all the powers seem to have vanished, and nothing is flowing. Writers can spend years out in the wilderness of blockland and never come back. Years waiting to finish that second novel – always hoping that they might. But books often urgently need to be written, and once they are, and are out of the head and onto the page and into the world, there's a huge relief. A moment's pause. But even that slow moment can be swiftly followed by extreme anxiety and worry about how the book might be received and reviewed, about whether or not the sham self will be found out and exposed and humiliated! (See? I told you: the writing life is not an easy life!)

## Jackie Kay

Jackie Kay was born to a Scottish mother and Nigerian father in Edinburgh on 9 November 1961, and was adopted as a baby by Helen and John Kay, who had already adopted a boy, Maxwell. The family lived in Bishopbriggs (Glasgow); John worked full time for the Communist Party of Great Britain, and Helen was the Scottish secretary of the Campaign for Nuclear Disarmament. Kay has drawn on her unconventional upbringing in her poetry, and described it with humour and great affection in her autobiographical account of the search for her birth parents, *Red Dust Road* (2010), which she has called a 'love letter' to her white adoptive parents.

# SCREEN DIVERSITY

## Shuchi Kothari

When I began film school in the US in 1990, within the first week I switched from the directing major to the writing major. Full of testosterone, the directing tutor shouted, "You've gotta be an asshole to be the director" and "You've gotta be the goddamned boss." I thought to myself "I'm not either of these things and it's not what I aspire to becoming." I went straight to the graduate adviser and asked if I could shift to screenwriting. He happened to be the head of the screenwriting area. He smiled and said, "I'm so glad because when I read your application I was hoping that you'd come to my side of the department." And I never regretted it. I've always loved screenwriting. I produce and direct projects too, but writing is my centre.

I also teach screenwriting at the University of Auckland and am director of the Screen Production programme. I have mentored short film and feature screenwriters and projects for Script to Screen and the New Zealand Film Commission. I have been an executive producer and co-producer on short films and features. I am one of the co-founders of the Pan-Asian Screen Collective (PASC), launched in 2017 to train, represent and advocate for Asian screen practitioners in Aotearoa/New Zealand. I have worked with Māori researchers and clinical practitioners in nursing, conducting community-based digital storytelling workshops with participants making films on *whānau* (family) care, and the customs and rituals around death and the dying. Irrespective of platform, storytelling is the beating heart of all my creative projects.

## THE WOMEN WRITERS' HANDBOOK

I have written critically acclaimed feature films: *Firaaq* (2008) with director Nandita Das; and *Apron Strings* (2008), co-written with Dianne Taylor and directed by Sima Urale. My short films include *Shit One Carries* (2018), which I wrote and directed; *Elder Birdsong* (Shuchi Kothari & Sarina Pearson, 2019), *Coffee and Allah* (Sima Urale, 2007); *Clean Linen* (Zia Mandviwalla, 2006); and *Fleeting Beauty* (Virginia Pitts, 2004). I was co-creator of *A Thousand Apologies* (TV3), a sketch-comedy show and New Zealand's first primetime Asian series. I was the writer and presenter of a documentary *The Taste of Place: Stories of Food and Longing* (TV1/TVNZ, 2001) and have just completed a highly collaborative eco-critical film about the desert in the Rann of Kutch in Gujarat.

I am eclectic, working across various screen forms and in several places. But there is a thematic connection across all my shorts and features, television work and academic publications. My writing always wrestles with ideas of home and belonging, inclusion, exclusion, language and marginality. My own difference/otherness is always in dialogue with the work I make. I'm interested in this struggle to belong or not belong; the choices that one makes or is allowed to make; the cost of adaptation, the loss of empowerment, structural racism, our relationship with *tangata whenua* (indigenous peoples of Aotearoa/New Zealand) and so on. And it is also important to acknowledge our varying privilege, so we don't conflate immigrants, migrants, exiles and refugees in one basket of diversity or minority. I always tell my writing students to render people's experiences with care and nuance; to commit to research, to collaborate (not simply consult) with communities of which you want to tell stories. For instance, Zahara Abbawaji, the lead actor in *Coffee & Allah*, came to Auckland as a refugee from Ethiopia via Kenya. I cannot pretend for a moment that my experience of displacement is the same as hers.

Language is such an integral part of how you understand characters or how they understand themselves. *Shit One Carries* has English, Gujarati and Hindi because that is often the linguistic reality of urban Gujarat. When I was writing Nandita Das's directorial debut *Firaaq*, characters spoke four languages and often code-switched. I'm currently writing another feature set in Ahmedabad that is also multilingual. So I've always been concerned about how we express ourselves as multilingual people, as transnationals working and living across places, between places sometimes and occasionally, lost in translation. Places and cultures are idiomatic and therefore some stories more naturally belong to them.

For people like me whose stories may be set here, or just as likely overseas, justifying "New Zealandness" is often painful. I strongly believe that if public funding mandates "New Zealand stories by New Zealanders" we need to deepen our understanding of New Zealanders and widen our definition of New Zealand stories. If you come from other places and become a Kiwi, your "other places" leave an imprint on you, on your being a New Zealander. I'm a Kiwi-Indian. I am this hyphenated person. Both places carry the other place.

Because we largely rely on public funding in the New Zealand context, it is doubly complicated for Asian screen practitioners. You can get stuck between a rock and a hard place. For some stories, the funders may say, "Yeah, but how can you make this work for all New Zealanders?" Whereas for other stories you may get, "Yeah, but what's Asian about this? We'd like you to use your voice." As an Asian do you always have to perform your Asianness? Who decides how Asian something really is? Or what does "all New Zealanders" mean? We have a lot of work to do in this area to create a more inclusive and representative screen.

The media industries have made it historically difficult for women directors and even harder for women of colour. My work involves collaborating with women filmmakers in particular. At some level in New Zealand all filmmakers struggle to create their own intellectual property in a small market in a small nation. But at the same time, there is something systemically faulty, if after Merata Mita's *Mauri* (1988), the first *wāhine* Māori-directed feature film was *Waru* (2017). The New Zealand on-air statistics for Asian creatives are woeful. We need public broadcasting so that certain narratives that ostensibly do not have market value are given an opportunity to find or create an audience.

In 2018, Selina Joe, Roseanne Liang, Gilbert Wong and I formed the Pan-Asian Screen Collective (PASC) to lobby for equitable opportunities for our young members, but also to point out structural blind spots within a system that has let these inequities flourish in the first place. Genuine "diversity" on screen should not be just about "showing different people", but the level of inclusivity in the processes of an organization, an environment and within systems of power.

Films are capital- and labour-intensive, so there is little point in developing projects without a clear sense of your audience. As I tell my students, a script is a blueprint for something that has yet to be made within an industrial context. An artist can paint just for themselves without ever showing their work to anyone. That's legitimate – the sketch in an artist's book is their completed work. But like most architects who design or sketch buildings that are yet to be constructed, screenwriters write screenplays knowing these are first links in a long industrial chain. Even though one can make a living in the USA optioning screenplays that never get made, their intention is always to see them fulfilled as films. Feature writing is a long road and can take something out of you, so if you're not interested in the audience then you're better off writing in a journal. Of course awareness of your audience should not be conflated with pandering to an audience. As a producer I have been on set a lot, and as a (occasional) director I am fascinated by that space in performance where the script leaves you, negotiating that space, being very much in that moment, not at all beholden to what is on the page but only to the emotion that the scene needs to convey.

If a film story gets written three times, first on the page, second time during performance, and the third in the edit, it's the very first flush of image and words that I find most exciting. Even though I know that the best version of my screenplay owes itself to several ruthless rewrites, the early harvest of ideas is delicate and tender (like a good Darjeeling tea) and requires careful handling. It's the memory of that feeling that helps me survive the hair-tearing moments of subsequent revisions.

What's not to love about writing? As the sportswriter Red Smith said in the 40s, "you simply sit down at the typewriter, open your veins, and bleed".

# WOMEN'S VOICES

**Shuchi Kothari**

Shuchi Kothari writes screenplays for the film industries in New Zealand, India, and USA. She has also produced short films of international acclaim and for television, New Zealand's first prime-time Asian show titled *A Thousand Apologies*.

Kothari's feature film *Firaaq* (2008) has screened at prestigious film festivals around the world, and has won 14 international awards. In 2010 Kothari was nominated in the "best story" category for the Star Screen Awards in India. Her creative work reflects her interest in issues related to migration, settlement, South Asian diaspora, and Indian cinema. She is the recipient of the New Zealand Film Commission's Writer's Award for 2009.

# WRITING PLAYS...

## Bryony Lavery

Imagine
An
Indian Bus Journey
...it starts off late
you run to catch it
someone throws you and all your baggage
through the open door
you're told it will take six hours
it takes twelve. and a half.
underpowered, overcrowded, fights break out
people get on to beg
you stop to get blessed at a shrine by the side of a road.
monkeys sit across the tarmac watching
with flat mean clever eyes call them critics
lots of meal stops, lots.
a cooking pan lid falls out at a crossroads.
We stop. It bowls away. Someone chases it, fetches it back.
Wedges it. A fight breaks out. Several small men
land hopeless too-little-protein punches on a ticket dodger.

## WOMEN'S VOICES

Ouch and ouch and oh it hurts but not seriously it's just a little bit of public shame.
A whole big chunk of underneath bus
breaks off, falls into the road.
The bus is broken. Everybody gets out.
Another bus. Get on.
Bus, underpowered, overweighted
climbs gasping, up the steep zigging and zagging
hill into clear mountain air
then, there's breathtaking, feel it, scenery
mountains, eagles, sky
an old single track railway toots through
and
you're high high high
up
Simla. A hill station.
Well, that's, bar several thousand miles, exactly
like
writing plays.

**Bryony Lavery**

Bryony Lavery's play *Frozen* won the TMA Best Play and the Eileen Anderson Central TV Awards and transferred from the National Theatre to Broadway, where it was nominated for four Tony awards. *Stockholm* won the Wolff-Whiting award for Best Play (2008). *Beautiful Burnout* (The National Theatre of Scotland/Frantic Assembly) received a Fringe First at Edinburgh, before productions in the UK, New York, Australia and New Zealand. *Dirt* was nominated for the Charles McArthur award for most outstanding play or musical of 2013, Washington DC. Lavery is a Fellow of The Royal Society of Literature, an honorary Doctor of Arts at De Montford University and an Associate Artist at Birmingham Rep. Theatre.

Artwork by Virginia Frances Sterrett

# THE NOVELIST AS WANDERER

## Annee Lawrence

Wandering is my approach to researching and writing a current novel – a work in progress that is inspired by the historian Jan Lingard's *Rebels and Refugees: Indonesian Exiles in Wartime Australia*. Lingard's book is an account of what happened, in World War II, when Australia set aside its infamous White Australia Policy to offer refuge to some 5,000 Indonesians. They came with the Dutch East Indies administration after it surrendered to the Japanese in 1942 and, more than a year later, some 500 political prisoners and their families were also transferred from Boven Digul, the region in Dutch New Guinea where they had been sent into exile by the colonial government. Their camp was known as Tanah Merah, Red Earth.

My interest in this story is linked to the light it sheds on a remarkable period of cross-cultural encounter and the offer of hospitality to strangers that resulted in many Australians, including some remarkable women, becoming active in the Indonesian struggle for independence on Australian soil. But for me as a writer, the volume of archival material about the intriguing characters – Dutch, Indonesian and Australian – and their often conflicted or conflicting agendas, the political power plays at national and international level, and the diverse activists in what unfolded, can seem both a blessing and a curse. It's like a jack-in-the-box: you open the lid and it resists all efforts to be pushed back down again.

So how do I as a writer engage with all this material? The challenge I face is to find a way – imaginatively and ethically – into the events that took place, while also making choices about characters, narrative structure and form. While the novel may draw on historical and social research, it must not be over-determined by it for it is a novel I am writing, and not a social history.

It seems then that I have no choice but to give myself over to following where the research, the writing and my imagination lead, and to delving into the gaps and silences in the archives and written accounts. That is, to treating the research and the text I am writing as though I were wandering in a foreign country, and where my responsibility as a visitor is to remain fluid, open and respectful of the strange and different along the way. It means setting aside the known and familiar, and moving by way of questioning, vulnerability and risk.

The question of what form the novel could or should take nips at my heels. Its initial shape is unwieldy and I try not to resist or reject it. In her essay 'The Vision Shared', the novelist Carson McCullers argues that the rejuvenation and revitalization of any artform is due to the numerous "single mutations" of creators whose new forms appear strange, or are misunderstood, when they first emerge, as any "growing things must go through awkward states". I take comfort from this observation as my novel continues to take shape in a curiously non-conventional, non-linear fashion, and I also take comfort from her assertion that "the creator who is misunderstood because of his breach of convention may say to himself, 'I seem strange to you, but anyway I am alive'".

Such writing appears intuitive. It unfolds in the process of being written, and by the way of wandering. And where in the writing, as McCullers refers to it, ideas and understandings come to the writer as *illuminations*, they may have an uncanny or even divine aspect which, while essential to the work, cannot be forced upon it. For McCullers the work is "like a flowering dream. Ideas grow, budding silently, and there are a thousand illuminations coming day by day as the work progresses". To illustrate, she describes how she worked on *The Heart is a Lonely Hunter* for a year – "without understanding it at all" – and how, when it finally came to her what the novel was, she became "for the first time committed with my whole soul to [it]."

What she means by being "committed" to the work is linked to the writer's (or any artist's) willingness to give herself over to the creative process, that is, over to the idea of writing as "a wandering creature". For McCullers, this also applies to the effect of the written work on the reader when it is read, such as when "a given passage or paragraph *draws astray* the imagination with sensual illusions, nuances of feelings, vibrations of memory and desire".

In my research for this novel I recognize that to write about my Indonesian teenage woman character I must know more about the internment camp in Boven Digul in Dutch New Guinea where she grew up, and where she and her family lived in indefinite detention. I wonder what life was like there, who the political prisoners were, how they got on, how they endured the poor diet and tropical illnesses and tried to remain sane. Then, what must it have been like to be transported to Australia, where they were placed in a prisoner-of-war camp in the middle of a bitterly cold winter? On arrival, their inability to cope with the cold, prior ill health and malnutrition, as well as their lack of immunity to common diseases, all combined to devastating effect when nine babies and adults succumbed and died. When I visit their graves I weep, and then later I weep again for the memory of it. At the same time, I recognize that there are uncanny resemblances in present-day Australia to the Dutch practice then, of exiling and interning people indefinitely and without trial, to an isolated and harsh faraway place.

In a cross-cultural novel in which the characters engage with one another and with everyday life, it may be that they have the potential to generate new cultures and literatures. This is an argument presented by Gabriele Schwab, in *Imaginary Ethnographies: Literature, Culture and Subjectivity,* who draws on Juan José Saer's (1997) definition of literature as "speculative anthropology" to highlight its "imaginary ways of remaking language and the world, shaping not only culture but also, and more directly, the cultural imaginary". By reading literary texts as "imaginary ethnographies", Schwab draws attention to the way they *"write culture* by inventing a language that redraws the boundaries of imaginable worlds and by providing *thick descriptions* of the desires, fears, and fantasies that shape the imaginary lives and cultural encounters of invented protagonists". As well as writing stories, Schwab argues, such texts "rewrite cultural narratives" and can be seen "as discourses and practices of cultural resistance".

## THE WOMEN WRITERS' HANDBOOK

Schwab also draws on Hans-Jörg Rheinberger's notion of "experimental systems" to argue for literature's capacity to use "language to explore, shape, and generate *emergent* forms of subjectivity, culture, and life in processes of dialogical exchange with its readers". For Schwab, this transforming power of literature is "less 'about' something than it is an embodied experience of something", and it takes place over time – even after the actual reading experience. Similarly, when a text is unfamiliar or strange, it demands of the reader that they "deal with their [own] otherness and foreignness", and this gives rise to "knowledge" that may be a "memorable and transformational experience of something that at this point escapes a full understanding or conceptual grasp".

The challenge for me as a novelist – when dealing with real historical events, places and people – is to allow the imagination to wander in the interstices between fact and fiction. But even so, it sometimes seems that there is too much light in this history and too much certainty and closure. Too many facts. Too many accounts.

Writing as a kind of truth and cultural form depends on the embodied relationship of the writer to the text she is writing. It is like a dialogue, a back-and-forth process between the writer and her text, in which she enters into a dialogue with her characters in a way Bakhtin characterizes as "polyphonic"; that is, as a dialogue between "equals where both parties enter into or, as he puts it, 'live into' each other". According to Celia Hunt and Fiona Sampson in *Writing: Self and Reflexivity*, such an approach, by its very nature, leaves the writer open to uncertainty and a continual questioning in relation to the agency of her characters.

In the to and fro of researching and writing, writing and researching, the writer submits to circumstance and language and, in the very choice of this area of research for my novel, I too encounter the poetics of double and multiple displacement that stretches my imaginative capacity and thrusts me into a constant state of uncertainty.

Language. Words. Sentences. Point of view. Character. Tension. Ambiguity. Form. Imagery. Metaphor. Narrative. Conflict. These are the tools carried in my pack as I wander into the cracks and crevices of history to realize the imagined lives of my characters. In my encounter with the alien and otherwise, in the sense that what I am writing is what history does not often tell, I am led to consider geographies, emotion, memory and time, as well as objects, relationships, nature, the human and non-human. And at every step of the way, there is a slow working together of cultures.

**Annee Lawrence**

Annee lives in Australia and has an interest in exploring cross-cultural connection. She has a PhD in creative writing and was the recipient of an Asialink Arts' inaugural Tulis Australian-Indonesian Writing Exchange in 2018. As a result, she had a six-week residency at Kommunitas Salihara in Jakarta and was invited to the Ubud Writers and Readers Festival. Prior to becoming a tutor in literary and cultural studies at Western Sydney University in 2014, Annee worked as a writer, editor and community development worker in the areas of women's health, human rights and social justice.

*The Colour of Things Unseen*, her debut novel, was published by Aurora Metro Books and launched at Ubud Writers and Readers Festival in Bali in 2019 and in Sydney, Australia in 2020.

anneelawrence.com

*"There is a fountain of youth: it is your mind, your talents, the creativity you bring to your life."*

– Sophia Loren

# INTERVIEW WITH ROSEANNE LIANG

Q. What do you enjoy most about being a writer?

A. I enjoy uncovering unexpected pleasures and truths – a line that makes me laugh, a blush of recognition with a character, a different perspective on our world. On a more macro level, for me, storytelling through the screen is a humanist communion. When I connect to other people's work, or people connect to my work, I feel less alone and less adrift in the cosmos.

Q. Is there anything you don't enjoy about being a writer?

A. It's funny – the very things I don't enjoy about screenwriting are often the same things that I end up seeking out again and again. I don't enjoy, for instance, how long it takes for me to actually start writing once I sit down: 2+ hours of procrastinatory internet surfing and self-flagellating social media checking before I even open Final Draft. What a miserably inefficient excuse for a writer I am. I don't enjoy how the same piece of my writing can suddenly change in perception, from a pat on the back for a job well done to a what-was-I-thinking piece-of-shit in the course of just one re-read. I don't enjoy feedback, still, but I need it. I don't enjoy that my first instincts aren't the best ones, and that I seem to need many iterations to get to the best ideas. I wish I was more of a spontaneous genius. I wish writing didn't take so long and wasn't so lonely. And yet I've come to find the loneliness necessary for meaningful writing.

# THE WOMEN WRITERS' HANDBOOK

Q. What's the best piece of professional advice you were given (creative or practical)?

A. Never work with anyone you wouldn't want to share a meal with." (credit to Tony Ayres)

"Be on time. You know what being late tells people? It tells people that you think your time is worth more than theirs." (credit to Michael Saccente)

Q. What motivates you to write?

A. Connecting to other people's work on screen. I'm inspired by the reckless, radical, revolutionary, boundary-pushing work that I'm watching, especially in TV drama. Sometimes I'm intimidated by the staggering craft that other screenwriters seem to effortlessly have; most other times it urges me to try and be as brave as they are.

Q. Do you have a favourite quotation from a book, poem, play or screenplay?

A. There are so many. Here's one from *Fleabag Season 2*. This battle cry is just one of the reasons why Phoebe Waller-Bridge feels so intimidatingly gifted:

"I've been longing to say this out loud. Women are born with pain built in. It's our physical destiny – period pains, sore boobs, childbirth. We carry it within ourselves throughout our lives. Men don't. They have to seek it out. They invent all these gods and demons so they can feel guilty about things, which is something we do very well on our own. And then they create wars so they can feel things and touch each other and when there aren't any wars they can play rugby. We have it all going on in here, inside. We have pain on a cycle for years and years and years, and then just when you feel you are making peace with it all, what happens? The menopause comes. The fucking menopause comes and it is the most wonderful fucking thing in the world. Yes, your entire pelvic floor crumbles and you get fucking hot and no one cares, but then you're free. No longer a slave, no longer a machine with parts. You're just a person. In business."

Q. How much of your own experience informs your writing?

## WOMEN'S VOICES

My experience, taste and instincts are all that I have when I write. The great thing is that I can always learn more, evolve my taste and develop better instincts.

**Q. What do you think about the argument that writers should only write material based on their own cultural background?**

A. I think that a dictum like this is reductive and requires deeper consideration case-by-case. As a child of Hong Kong immigrants, born in New Zealand, I grew up on myriad cultural influences including a steady diet of US and British film and TV. Could I write a Hollywood film? Sure, with the right team. A BBC TV series? Absolutely, if I did my homework. Do I think non-Maori should write Maori stories? Well – let's talk about that. Issues of representation and decolonization are necessarily complex and need to bring into account the system that we exist in, and have existed in for decades with regard to modern screenwriting. If, for instance, a small percentage of New Zealand stories written are Maori stories, and if most of that small percentage of Maori stories are being written by non-Maori writers, and produced by non-Maori producers, then I think we have a problem.

**Q. What's the best decision you've made in your writing career (creative or practical)?**

A. To set up a writing space away from my home. I acknowledge this is a huge privilege. I thank the gods every day for a space where I can retreat to be alone with my thoughts.

**Q. What advice would you give to a new writer?**

A. Everything they say about following your gut, finding your voice, tenacity, hard work and working consistently on a body of work and closing the gap between your own killer taste and what you are making, is true. All the things you've heard about meditation and exercise are also true.

# THE WOMEN WRITERS' HANDBOOK

**Roseanne Liang**

Roseanne Liang is a New Zealand-born Chinese director and screenwriter. Her autobiographical feature film *My Wedding and Other Secrets* was the top-grossing NZ-made film in the year of its release. Roseanne has also made award-winning work across TV comedy and short film including Berlin-winning *Take 3*, cult-favourite webseries *Flat3/Friday Night Bites*, and Sundance-SXSW breakout action short *Do No Harm*. Tipped in the *Hollywood Reporter* and *The Alice Initiative* as one to watch, she is completing her debut US action-thriller feature film called *Shadow in the Cloud*, starring Chloe Grace Moretz and Nick Robinson.

# MEI KWEI, I LOVE YOU[1]

## Suchen Christine Lim

### 1

Two hours past midnight, Cha-li was sitting inside her grey Toyota, watching the corner house in Sennett Estate. There were nights when she wanted to call it quits, but she didn't because she'd given her word. Keeping her word was essential in her business. It was what drew women to her. The scarred, the abused, the cheated, the exploited, the rejects and the victims. Single or married, they came to her at the temple. They knew by word-of-mouth that her specialty was adultery and infidelity. Not for her – the commercial investigations or surveillance of employees or insurance fraud or missing persons. A specialist in unfaithfulness, that's what you are, a client had told her. Cha-li liked the phrase. It made her feel she was more than a private eye. She was the PI who peered into hearts seething with dark secrets and contradictions. But she was cautious about making any claims. A private investigator deals with hard facts – the what, the when and the where – not the speculative whys and wherefores. That was what she told Robina Lee, who'd come to see her two weeks ago.

"Where is Charlie Wong?" Robina had asked in a peremptory voice.

"I am Cha-li Wong," she answered as confusion clouded the young woman's eyes. Cha-li was used to such reactions. Before meeting her in person, many people thought her Mandarin name, Cha-li (Beautiful Guard), was Charlie, because they'd expected the investigator to be a guy.

[1] First published in *Singapore Noir* edited by Cheryl Lu Lien Tan, Akashic Books, New York, 2014.

## THE WOMEN WRITERS' HANDBOOK

Just like they'd expected a guy to take over as the medium of Lord Sun Wukong's temple. Ah well, such things no longer bothered her.

"Robina Lee," the woman introduced herself. "Not my married name," she added, and sat down across from Cha-li, who reckoned her age to be thirty or so. Robina was tanned, slim, and looked tense. Her lips were rouged a deep pink, and her eyes had dark rings around them. Cha-li noted the smart black stilettos and expensive black leather handbag, and wondered if Robina was one of those high-flying execs from the towering offices in Shenton Way. The look that Robina gave her seemed haughty at first. Seated with legs crossed and hands clenched tightly around the arms of the chair, she said in pitch-perfect Mandarin, "My husband is seeing another woman. I would like to engage your services to find out who the woman is. What hold she has on him. What black magic," and here Robina switched to the Hokkien dialect and said emphatically, "what *kong tau* the vixen used to ensnare him. I need a private investigator and a medium. I'm told you're both. I will pay you well above market rates if you agree to handle the case."

Taken aback, Cha-li muttered that she'd stopped conducting séances. She was more of a caretaker than a medium of the temple these days. "No matter," Robina Lee said, and would not take no for an answer. She desperately needed a private investigator with knowledge of the black arts and *kong tau*. But what proof did she have that her husband had eaten *kong tau*? Cha-li asked. Robina stared at her hands, still clenched. Her husband was always distracted at home after dinner each night. At times he was glassy-eyed, distant and vague. He shot out of the house the moment his mobile rang. The family's business and reputation were suffering. But that did not necessarily prove he was bewitched, Cha-li pointed out. Robina's voice rose. "Proof? You want proof? Then you tell me. Why else would a young man desert his young wife for a woman old enough to be his mother? Look at me. I am not yet thirty!"

Cha-li calmed her down, agreed that it was an uncommon case. Far more common for a man to leave his old wife for a young mistress. But as a private investigator, she had to suspend judgement. Observe, listen, gather and assemble the facts, objects, people and events without adding or subtracting, explaining or interpreting. That should be the PI's objective,

## WOMEN'S VOICES

she explained to Robina. The temple medium, on the other hand, could go beyond the realm of fact and information to things hovering in the shadows, at the corner of one's eye.

"Look, I don't care what you do. Just be discreet. I will pay you well." Those were Robina Lee's parting words.

\*

A black cat jumped onto the bonnet of Robert Lee's white Mercedes and disappeared down the other side. Cha-li glanced at her watch. 2:38 a.m. Is he spending the night in the corner house? Could he be so bold as to leave his car parked in front of the house till morning? She rolled down her window and settled in to wait the whole night.

Butterfly Avenue was hushed, and the air was cool under the thick canopy of trees and bush. All the houses down the road had switched off their lights except the corner house at the end of the row of two-storey terraces, each with a fenced-in garden, driveway and a car under the porch, the symbols that spelled middle class and private property ownership. Cha-li doubted she'd ever be able to own one of these prim-looking terraces. She was familiar with this private housing estate known as Sennett Estate in Potong Pasir, which had made history when it voted in Singapore's sole opposition MP in 1984. A teenager then, she saw how Prime Minister Lee Kuan Yew tore into and shredded the academic record of the opposition candidate, Chiam See Tong, and that had so roused the residents of Potong Pasir that they voted for the underdog. That year her heart had swelled with pride as she watched Kai-yeh, her adoptive father and medium of the Lord Sun Wukong's temple, rally the villagers to vote for Mr Chiam. 1984 was also the year she crossed Upper Serangoon, the busy main road that separated her village from wealthy Sennett Estate, to attend Cedar Girls' School, not far from Butterfly Avenue.

She reached for the night-vision binoculars in her glove box and trained them on the house at the corner. The front door had opened and two figures had emerged. Robert Lee was with a woman silhouetted against the light from the living room. The woman was laughing and pushing him toward the gate. Cha-li's heart stopped. She couldn't breathe. Is that Rose? But Rose was dead. Died in Macau. That was what her sources had told her years ago. Were they wrong? Cha-li watched the woman in the red housecoat open the gate, push Mr Lee out, and shut it. Her eyes following the woman's retreating figure, she failed to catch the sound of a car engine starting. She didn't even see the white Mercedes drive away. Something was unravelling inside her head.

*Mei kwei, Mei kwei, wo ai ni.*

*Rose, Rose, I love you.*

A song she hadn't heard for years.

\*

They had grown up together, she and Rose, in Lord Sun Wukong's temple in Potong Pasir village. She was the medium's adopted daughter, while Rose was the unwanted mewling waif fished out of the temple's bucket latrine. Throughout their childhood, Rose was caned often, while she, Cha-li, was spoiled rotten by Kai-ma, her adoptive mother, and Kai-yeh, her adoptive father, who channelled the spirit of Lord Sun Wukong, the Monkey King.

In those days, Potong Pasir was a stinking labyrinth of filthy lanes, muddy ponds, duck and vegetable farms, attap huts and outhouses with bucket latrines. The latrine is in your flesh! Kai-ma railed at Rose. Go and bathe, you filthy rag! But no matter how often Rose took a bath, she could never shake off the stench that seemed to seep into her clothes, her hair and under her skin. Rose cursed the mother who gave birth to her and dumped her in the temple's outhouse. The children teased her. Sai! Sai! They yelled in Hokkien. Even the adults called her Ah Sai – 'lump of shit'. The village boys would kick open the door of the outhouse whenever Rose was crouched inside. One day, Cha-li heard a loud quacking and flapping of wings. The bullies had jumped into the duck pond, splashing and yelling as they frantically washed themselves – evidently Rose had suddenly opened the outhouse door and hurled several brown lumps at them. "You are the sai! Not me! I am Rose the beautiful!" she screeched. Cha-li laughed.

Rose ran away from the temple several times, away from the stink and choke of joss and other incense. Away from Kai-ma's caning and the boys' taunting. But the trail of rot pursued her wherever she went. The faster she ran, darting this way and that among the huts, the more lost she felt. Sometimes Cha-li found her crying in Yee Soh's outhouse with the mangy bitch snarling outside. Sometimes Rose hid under the bushes after Kai-ma had caned her. Once Cha-li found her on Upper Serangoon Road, a wiry urchin gulping exhaust fumes from the city's buses as though they were fresh air. The fumes overwhelmed the stench in her flesh, Rose said, her eyes bright as stars. The world outside Potong Pasir was a heady mix of new smells, speed and ceaseless motion to her. She gripped Cha-li's arm. "Run!" she yelled, and pulled Cha-li along. Cars honked as they dashed across the busy road, dodging bicycles, motorcycles, hawkers' carts and trishaws ferrying women and children.

Once across, Rose demanded: "How much you have in your pocket? Show me. Come on, you monkey." She twisted Cha-li's arm. "I know you've got money in your pocket." Her nails dug into Cha-li's flesh until she cried out. Then all of a sudden she felt Rose's hand stroking her face. "Don't cry, little monkey, please don't cry." A thrill shot through Cha-li's heart. It was pounding so hard against her rib cage she had to shut her eyes to stop the dizziness coursing through her, the better to savour the sensuous feel of Rose's hand on her cheek. She took out all the coins in her pocket and dropped them into Rose's hand.

"I knew it! You little monkey! Forty cents! Let's go and buy *tau huey*!"

Sweet bean curd was Rose's favourite dessert. She ate tubs of it in those half-forgotten days, which was why her skin was so smooth and fair, and smelled so sweet that Cha-li almost swooned when Rose held her in the kitchen the night they both turned fifteen. "Prostitutes!" Kai-ma's broom hit them on their heads. Rose sprinted out of the kitchen, and didn't return for three days and three nights.

\*

## THE WOMEN WRITERS' HANDBOOK

Cha-li sighed, and returned the binoculars to her glovebox feeling as if she had crawled out of a black hole where time had warped like a rattan mat left in the sun too long. How long had she been sitting in the car lost in her own thoughts? She was ashamed. This was uncharacteristic. And worse, she'd lost her quarry. Robert Lee's white Mercedes was gone. The gate of the corner house was shut, and the woman who looked like Rose had disappeared back inside. The house stood in darkness. Butterfly Avenue was wrapped in silence at three a.m. The night air was soft and sweet, as though this avenue was not part of such a densely populated city, as though it belonged to a time when there were few cars, and migrant workers from China, India or Bangladesh hadn't yet squeezed Singaporeans out of the crowded buses and trains.

She took out her black notebook, wrote down the time, date and her observations, and then shut it. It pained her to think of what she'd tell Robina Lee the next day. The woman had phoned earlier to say that she was coming to the temple tomorrow. Cha-li had no wish to see her yet, but an operative must maintain close contact with her client, just as a medium must maintain close psychic contact with the spirit she is channelling.

She got out of the car. She had to clear her head. She walked past the corner house and followed the road beyond the silent, gated bungalows, their orange roofs gleaming in the ghostly night sky. There was no moon. Just banks of ominous grey clouds. Her mind returned to the woman who looked like Rose. If it was Rose, what was she doing back here? Has she moved up in the world through Robert Lee, son of a hotel chain tycoon? Is he her young lover? Is he bankrolling her?

Information was scarce at this point. Robina Lee was reluctant to tell her more. You are the investigator. You find out, she'd said at their last meeting. And let me remind you of your high fee plus expenses. In return, I expect the strictest confidence.

Cha-li grimaced at the memory of that voice. No, she didn't want to see Robina Lee tomorrow, and looked up, surprised that her feet had led her to the gate of Cedar Girls' School. She must have turned onto Cedar Avenue without thinking. This was their secondary school before Rose was expelled for what the school called "unhealthy relationships".

## WOMEN'S VOICES

"Monkey!" Rose had yelled on the first day of school. "Did you see the school toilet? No shit! No flies! No smell! So clean! You just pull the metal chain. And whooooosh! The water flushes away everything!" Rose's face was glowing. "The toilets aren't like those in Potong Pasir village," she said. "When I grow up I want to live in a beautiful house with a clean toilet just like this."

"And me? What about me?" Cha-li asked.

"Oh, you? You will live in the temple, *lor*! You will be Lord Sun Wukong's medium."

"No," Cha-li protested. But it was not a very strong protest.

She turned away from the school and returned to Butterfly Avenue. A dog barked at her, strident and querulous. Cha-li crossed over to the other side of the road, just so the stupid Alsatian wouldn't wake up the neighbourhood. The avenue was U-shaped, and where it curved, there was a small playground with a slide and a swing under the trees. Their shadows fell across the park where a girl's soft giggles broke the night's calm. She saw a young Rose and herself on the swing. Rose was pushing her higher and higher, and she was laughing and screaming, "Stop! Stop!"

What must you say? What must you say?

*"Mei kwei, Mei kwei, wo ai ni."*

"Rose, Rose, I love you."

The Alsatian's barking grew louder, joined now by the yelpings of other dogs. She quickened her pace. Just as she was about to reach her grey Toyota, a glimpse of black hair caught her attention. Near the red car. No, the black one. No. It's a mirage. An optical illusion. She must be hallucinating. Go home, Cha-li. Go get some sleep!

She parked her Toyota in the wasteland next to the canal, formerly known as the Kallang River that meandered through Potong Pasir village in the old days. Wild grass, bush and creepers grew around the old temple. The wasteland became a fairground every August during the feast of the Monkey King when an open-air stage was erected and a street opera was performed for the gods and devotees. When Kai-yeh was the medium, the entire village of Potong Pasir would gather at the temple to pray, eat and watch street opera for three days and three nights. These days, however, like the slow-flowing Kallang River that had given way to the rapid Kallang Canal, the street operas had given way to *getai* in which scantily clad women sang and danced, not for the gods but for the younger devotees who loved MTV. The wasteland had also shrunk, and the concrete blocks of apartments had moved closer to the temple each year.

2

She parked her car and went into the temple, surprised to find Robina Lee among the women praying at the altar of the Monkey King.

"Good morning, Wong Sifu," the women greeted her.

In their eyes, she would always be Sifu or Master Wong, who channelled the spirit of the Monkey King. That she was also a private investigator was irrelevant to them; it was just a job to fill her rice bowl. Periodically, she suffered pangs of unease. She was a fraud burdened by a sacred duty that had been imposed on her as a child. As the chosen one, selected by Kai-yeh, who had consulted the Monkey King's spirit before anointing her as his successor, she had to serve in his absence. Years of performing the rituals, the chanting and the comforting, had won her scores of grateful devotees, women who respected and adored her. Some had even been her lovers when she was young, handsome, lonely and pining for Rose.

"Good morning, Sifu!" the women called out to her again.

"Good morning, good morning!" she said, laughing as she opened the door to her office. Robina followed her inside and closed the door. She was wearing a dark pantsuit and sunglasses. When she took off her glasses, Cha-li saw the wretched look in her eyes. Her face was puffy, and there was a dark bruise on her right temple.

"Did your husband do this?"

Robina shook her head, and Cha-li didn't press her. "He slept in the baby's room last night. He didn't want me near him." Robina's voice was flat. "You must give me a ritual cleansing. Please."

# WOMEN'S VOICES

Shocked by the request, Cha-li tried to focus her attention on the case instead.

"I have checked out your husband's new office in Shenton Way. His clients are all Indians. Rich fat cats who are buying up our luxury condos."

"Robert is repulsed by the sight of me."

"He's running some kind of consultancy that includes real estate."

"Help me, Wong Sifu," Robina pleaded, kneeling suddenly.

"No, no, please. Please stand up."

"Our little boy is only six months old. Robert owes people a lot of money. My father-in-law does not know it yet. I fear... I..."

"Wait, Robina. I know. I ran a check—"

"He's bewitched. It's that vixen. Please, Wong Sifu, help me. The family... the... the scandal will ruin his father. Please, Sifu!"

Cha-li sighed. She was hoping it wouldn't lead to this. "Go into the prayer hall, Robina. I have to change."

She did not move until the woman had left the room. Then she locked the door.

The anointed are never free. They must respond to the cries of the broken and lost — Kai-yeh had drilled this into her from a young age. They sought her, these broken hearts. She had tried to tell them that Lord Sun Wukong, the Monkey King, was a figment of an author's imagination in 16th century Ming China, but all to no avail. Besides, there were the women's testimonies. *Lord Sun Wukong answered my prayers*, some claimed. *He granted me a son*, declared another. *He made my husband stop seeing that woman and come back to me.*

She sighed. The women's beliefs had tinted their perceptions and shaped their universe; Lord Sun Wukong was the godly spirit who came to their aid. If she was tempted at times to tell them to pray to a rock, which would work just as well, she restrained herself. If praying had helped these women to sit still long enough for their problems to work themselves out, what right had she to destroy their faith in something higher than themselves? No bloody right at all! She yanked off her blue jeans and pulled on a pair of gold-coloured silk pants. Then she took off her red checked blouse and slipped on a white silk shirt and the Monkey King's bronze headband. She gazed at the woman in the mirror, dressed in silk pyjamas.

Would her features turn simian when she was as old as Kai-yeh?

She was six when Lord Sun Wukong, through the intercession of Kai-yeh, chose her to be his young messenger. Thrilled and scared that she, and not Rose, was the Chosen One, she had knelt before his altar and drunk a cup of tea mixed with holy joss ash. Lord Sun Wukong was a wise, courageous, shape-changing god in the Taoist pantheon of deities, Kai-yeh told her. Capable of forty-nine changes; he could change himself into a fly, a beautiful woman, a monster or a rock at the blink of an eye. That's what I want to do, she declared. Kai-yeh laughed: That you will, my child. That you will.

Later, in school, she discovered that the English storybooks referred to the deity as the Monkey King. In the temple, however, he was respectfully addressed as Lord Sun Wukong. His altar was covered with a red velvet ceremonial tablecloth embroidered with the Eight Immortals. The cloth reached down to the floor, hiding anyone under the altar from view. That was where she and Rose had slept as teenagers, hugging each other close each night, especially after Kai-ma's death, when Rose refused to sleep in the kitchen alone. Kai-yeh sleepwalks and touches me, she complained.

The temple's drum boomed. Her assistant called out in a loud voice: "Make way for His Excellency, Lord Sun Wukong!"

Cha-li took her rod and glided into the prayer hall.

3

The following week, on Monday evening, she waited in the parking lot of Tower Block One, Shenton Way. Outside, a thunderstorm was pelting the city hard. After two weeks of blistering sunshine and high humidity that caused her shirts to cling to her back, the weather had finally turned. The storm raged as she sat in her car, watching Lift Lobby Two and the white Mercedes parked near it. Robert Lee should appear at any moment. By seven, the storm petered out. Several men and women walked out of the lift, got into their cars, and drove off, leaving large gaps between the remaining cars. Bored, she continued to keep an eye on movements in the lift lobby as a light drizzle started to fall on the city's gray towers now gleaming wet in the lamplight. Another hour passed, and still no sign of Robert Lee. Lift Lobby Two was brightly lit and empty, most of the executives having left the building by now.

For the past two weeks, Robert had left his office between six and seven. Tonight he was late, but he could dash out of the lift any minute. Two evenings ago, she'd had to duck her head and pretend she was reaching for something in the backseat when he'd come out of the lift suddenly with an Indian client in tow. Tonight she was better prepared. She had donned a wig and changed her glasses.

At 8:46 p.m. Robert Lee came out of the lift, alone. He drove out of the parking lot with Cha-li tailing him through heavy traffic to Orchard Road and the Hilton. She did not follow him into the hotel this time. Instead, she drove home to collect Saddam Hussein. Tonight she would try a new strategy.

At 10 p.m. she parked her grey Toyota near the playground on Butterfly Avenue and got out.

"Come on, Saddam boy. Okay, okay! Let's go!"

Her fox terrier jumped out of the car, pulling at its leash. Laughing, Cha-li jogged after Saddam Hussein – taking the dog out at night was a good camouflage. Running down the lanes gave her a chance to observe the corner house on Butterfly Avenue from different vantage points. She could see a pattern beginning to emerge.

As she came round the corner, Robert Lee's white Mercedes stopped in front of the corner house. His passenger, a well-groomed Indian male in a long-sleeved blue shirt and dark trousers, stepped out and pressed the buzzer on the gate. When it opened, Robert Lee drove off.

Back inside her grey Toyota with Saddam Hussein panting in the backseat, she checked her notes again. For the past several nights, Robert Lee had brought a different Indian male to the house. Sometimes, Robert went in with his guest. But last Tuesday night, he had dropped his Indian guy off and driven away, and she had tailed him back to his home. Last

## THE WOMEN WRITERS' HANDBOOK

Monday, Wednesday and Friday nights, Robert had parked his car and followed his Indian guest into the house. About two hours later, the two men had returned to the car and driven back to the Indian's hotel. Just this week alone, she had followed Robert to several high-end hotels. On Monday night, it was the Fullerton. On Wednesday night, it was Marina Bay Sands. On Friday night, the Ritz-Carlton. On Saturday night, the Shangri-La. But all these details hardly spelled adultery. Robert Lee was simply the chauffeur for his rich Indians. She'd not seen any women coming out of the corner house yet, except the one in red who looked like Rose. She flipped over several more pages in her notebook. Nothing important in there. Her surveillance of Robert's office had yielded little except a list of his dinner appointments with Indian clients, who inevitably ended up going to the corner house for dessert. Which was interesting. Is the house a brothel? Unlikely. Butterfly Avenue was not Geylang Road. Sennett Estate was in one of the city's respectable middle-class areas. It's true that some wealthy Chinese had bought houses here for their mistresses, but this had not dented the estate's respectability. Besides, she had not seen any young women emerging from the corner house. Was the woman in red the sole magnet that attracted the Indians? But if the woman was Rose, she'd be fifty-five and considered over the hill, no? Unless... unless she was offering something kinky.


4


Cha-li parked the rental van outside the corner house. Pulling a cap on her head, she got out, pressed the buzzer on the gate, and shouted into the intercom, "*Karang guni!* Collect old newspapers!"

The gate opened, and she walked up the driveway. The front door was ajar.

"Come in!" a woman shouted from the kitchen.

Cha-li stepped inside the spacious living room. Its walls were apple white, and the floor was of white marble. A large white sofa and two armchairs upholstered in white leather sat on a thick beige and grey

## WOMEN'S VOICES

carpet. The woman who came out of the kitchen didn't seem surprised to see her.

"Rose." That was all Cha-li could manage. Her throat was dry.

Rose, meanwhile, said nothing. She had not moved from her spot near the kitchen. Cha-li peered at her. Wearing a pink housecoat, she looked like the aunties who came to the temple to pray. At fifty-five, Rose was no longer the young, dark, beauty queen who had held men spellbound as she gyrated onstage with a python in the Great World Cabaret and broke her heart. A hard glint appeared in Rose's eyes as she looked at Cha-li, who searched for something to say now that she was face to face with the girl – no, the woman – she had once loved.

Scenes from their past came and went in her head. She saw their two naked bodies, tinted red by sunlight shining through the red tablecloth covering Lord Sun Wukong's altar, as Rose's fingers reached into the deep moist recesses between her thighs, stirring feelings of love, guilt and shame. Ashamed of what she felt, and conscious that she was Kai-yeh's chosen successor while Rose was just the temple's waif, she had fought hard to suppress her feelings. Until one day, Rose was gone. Gone without a word. Frantic with worry, and sobbing her heart out, she went to the police. A missing person's report was filed but nothing came of it. She wept long and hard every night. For months she haunted the places they used to visit. Kai-yeh was philosophical. Rose is a temple stray. Strays come and go. It's their nature, he said, and encouraged her to study hard.

Five years later, she became a private investigator. She was on duty in the Malaysian town of Ipoh when she chanced upon a large black-and-white photo of Rose in the Great World Cabaret. It showed a scantily clad sultry beauty with long, dark tresses and a large python curled around her. Shocked, she sat through Rose's show before charging into her dressing room backstage.

"Fuck off, Cha-li! I don't owe you an explanation! The cabaret! Now, that's *my* temple! It's where I dance like a woman. Sexy and beautiful. You! You prance around that temple like a dressed-up monkey!" Stung, Cha-li left the cabaret, and hadn't seen Rose again.

"You might as well take off the cap."

## THE WOMEN WRITERS' HANDBOOK

Cha-li pulled off her cap and stuffed it into the pocket of her jeans.

"Why have you come?" Rose asked in a hard voice.

"Kai-yeh is dying."

"Good! May he rot in hell!"

"He gave you a roof over your head, Rose."

"Keep your pious shit, Cha-li. You're blind, and a fool. He gave me more than that. Come."

Cha-li followed her into the kitchen. Rose threw open a door, and Cha-li walked into the kitchen of the house next door. She followed Rose into the dining room where an old woman was trying unsuccessfully to feed a young man strapped to his chair. The young man's large shaved head was lolling on the back of the chair as though his neck was too soft to support it. Spit was dribbling from the corner of his mouth, which was making guttural sounds. The old woman wiped off the spit with a washcloth, and shoved another spoonful of rice into the gaping hole as though to stop the ugly sounds coming from it.

"Ugh! Ugh! Ugh!"

"What your Kai-yeh gave me."

Cha-li stared at the head and vacant eyes. "Did he...? Did he...?" Helpless, she turned to Rose."He raped me. Then I tried to abort him." Rose patted the lolling head, which said, "Ugh! Ugh!" and more spit dribbled.

"Good morning, Madame Mei Kwei! Good morning, Ugh-Ugh!" two girls called out in Mandarin as they came down the stairs, their nipples showing under their skimpy nightdresses.

Cha-li remembered seeing them when she was walking Saddam Hussein. One of the girls approached them and planted a kiss on the lolling head.

"Ugh! Ugh!" The distended mouth dribbled more spit, and the wrists strained at the belt that strapped them to the armrests.

Rose turned away. "Let's go back. They're getting ready to eat."

## WOMEN'S VOICES

Cha-li followed her back to the first house. The sun had come into the living room, and the light that bounced off the white marble floor hurt her eyes. Her head was swimming.

"Is Robert the mastermind?"

"No. Robert has to settle his gambling debts. I... ah! I need the money and so do these China girls. They have something to sell that the Indians want to buy. Robert brings the Indians. I bring the girls. Everyone is happy. It's not a crime."

"I don't know about that."

Rose drew the curtains. "Report it to the police if you want. I don't care what you do."

"Why? Why didn't you tell me what he did?"

"Tell you?" Rose's laughter bordered on the hysterical, a wild gleam in her eyes. "Tell *you*? The bastard's monkey girl? The Great Lord's Chosen One with a paper gold band on your head? And a fake gold chain around your neck? The bastard was holding the bloody chain while you pranced before the devotees, drunk in their adoration. Strike me dead, Cha-li! I couldn't tear open my heart and offer it to a prancing monkey in silk robes!"

She wanted to slap Rose but walked to the front door instead and stopped at the doorway, surprised at the sudden weight in her limbs. Her shoulders sagged. The memory of the gilt headband that she'd worn in those days made her cringe. It was made of cardboard and cheap plastic, painted gold. Later, she had bought the bronze headband to replace it.

The sunlight outside hurt her eyes, which were beginning to tear, the same eyes that had remained shut when footsteps were shuffling in the middle of the night into the kitchen where Rose slept. Rose's mouth was moving, saying something to her but she couldn't catch the words. She kept thinking of the lolling head and dribbling mouth next door.

"The... the temple will be demolished. Very soon," she said without turning around. She couldn't face Rose. She wanted to shut her eyes, shut out the noonday glare, but she forced herself to keep them open, fixed on the green lawn outside, sizzling in the midday heat.

"I... I can get a flat big enough for the three... three of us... er... you and him..." Her voice trailed off.

## THE WOMEN WRITERS' HANDBOOK

*This story was a finalist in the Private Eye Writers of America Shamus Award 2015*

**Suchen Christine Lim**

In 2012, Lim was named the Singapore recipient of the South East Asia Write Award. Her most recent novel, *The River's Song*, was published by Aurora Metro Books (2014) and was named 'Best Books of 2015' by Kirkus Reviews. Her novel *Fistful of Colours* (1992) was awarded the Inaugural Singapore Literature Prize. A short story from Lim's *The Lies That Build A Marriage*, was made into a film. Her work is also featured in *Writing The City*, commissioned by British Council, Singapore.

She has received a Fulbright grant, and is also a Fellow and former International Writer-in-Residence of the International Writers' Program, University of Iowa. She was the Arvon Foundation writer-in-residence, at Moniack Mhor, in 2005. She has participated in the Edinburgh Book Festival and the Melbourne Writers' Festival, among many others. Lim has also held writing residencies in the Philippines, Myanmar, South Korea, Australia and the United Kingdom.

*"I can shake off everything as I write; my sorrows disappear, my courage is reborn."*

— Anne Frank

Artwork by Colleen O'Dell

# THE BADMINTON COURT

## Jaki McCarrick

The window of my room faces a tall hedge and an ancient oak, home to a kestrel and her two chicks. Beyond Redwood are hills, the edge of a winding silver lake. As I observe its gleam curl around the estate, I know instantly that I do not have to cross the lake to find what I need, that happiness is a small question, easily answered.

Summer. The smell of cut grass, the faint odour of plimsolls. Throughout the house the unmistakable bouquet of hemp. Fourteen acres of manicured gardens and lawns. The sky an azure spell. Clouds that are bird-shaped: an eagle, doves, buzzards. There is a palpable sense of waiting on the badminton court below, a silence soon to be punctured by bat whacks, whistling shuttlecocks and the swish of serge skirts.

I look down at the court, the sun scalding the lawn, the bullfinches gathering in the gods of the low, long hedge to watch the morning game. I know I'll be here for a while. Then music: Saint-Saëns, Joy Division. I know what she wants. I hear the front door slam. I go to the games room and change into the maroon-coloured gown. I am here to play. I am here to help her forget. I am here to help her die.

This is Redwood House, Suffolk. Constable country. Miranda is seventeen. She is thin with shorn blonde hair, and is altogether the most disarmingly honest person I have ever met. Reveals to everyone precisely what her illness is, gives them diagnosis and prognosis. Brain tumour. Malignant. Grade four. Three to six months. I am used to a more guarded (though perhaps "duplicit" is a better word) environment. My father's

## WOMEN'S VOICES

cagey manoeuvres, his dubious schemes, his admired business acumen. My presence is itself the settlement of his debts to Miranda's father.

Apart from Frances and me, she is alone at Redwood. Her father is off on some protracted business trip; her mother, never discussed, is, I think, barely known to her. The herbal preparations, the meals, the thrice-weekly trips to the clinic, are left to Frances.

Further to the south of Redwood there is another property, with a small boathouse: South Lodge. Lavender hedgerows, saxifrage-covered rocks, an assortment of mangy cats and kittens. This is Inshaw's place. From this land he watches us. When we play, he pretends he is out gathering mushrooms or repairing the corrugated roof of the boathouse. Sometimes I see his dark, deliquescent eyes follow the shuttlecock back and forth over the net. He is a presence in the game; triangulates it. She tells me to ignore him.

I have become, within weeks, father and mother to her. Father, mother and more.

Dinner. Frances has prepared salmon and marinated tuna and Miranda wants to teach me how to use chopsticks. As I practise the pincer-like movement, I notice how she rests one of the sticks against her fat bottom lip. I am jealous of it, nestled in that soft place. She rises, comes towards me. The sick smell of her as she bends over my shoulder; death is in her breath. I have forgotten she is so ill. It is easy to do: that lightness of spirit, precision of play. She drops her head on my hair. Your beautiful hair, she says, your long, dark beautiful hair. I am aware of her bones against my own tumescence and curves. She comes away, stands before me, androgynous and stark, and for a moment it seems as if each of us has been called up from the depths of the other's consciousness. We go on like this. The days are endless, summer does not turn. Only I notice the chicks are bigger in the oak, and that Inshaw has finally repaired his roof and is sailing his boat, or I would hardly register the passing of time at all.

I bump into Inshaw in the village. I am surprised. Nice man, shy. We discuss Miranda. Poor Miranda. It isn't fair. It isn't right. He says he will look out for her when I leave at the end of September. I realize I do not want to leave, not ever. I think of my first night and the thoughts I'd had of escape, of secret instant escape onto the tall hedge; I consider how fortunate it was I did not give in to those thoughts. The encounter with Inshaw has startled me. The sudden reality of the situation, a splint of cold glass in my skull.

She says little at breakfast. The evening before, she had been on fire. Rapid, erratic thoughts, unfinished sentences, sentences that unravelled, ending in lacunae, gibberish. She had been rude, her inhibitors obstructed by that thing, growing, multiplying inside her. Tumour talk, Frances calls it. She has some toast, a thimble of marmalade, tea. I know she wants a game because she is dressed in the maroon gown. Worn when badminton was played as formally as tennis or cricket, the serge gowns are almost a hundred years old. They belonged to her grandmother. Miranda had found them soot-soaked in the cellar, later began to wear one as protection from the sun. Long-sleeved, cuffed, mandarin-collared, they are oriental in design. Frances says they make us seem like twins. Miranda leaves the house and I go to the games room to change. She has left a sprig of something – eglantine – by my washed and ironed gown on the bench. The sight of it horrifies me.

Our last game. Her play is at half-speed. Her co-ordination off. She is all over the place, drops the shuttlecock. It is tragic to watch. She observes the weakness in her own swing. Summons all her strength and it is poor. Flails about with the racket, pretends there is something wrong with it, but her racket is fine. Essays an awkward thrust and teeters. She is being milked by that thing. It is unspeakable. Eventually she gets a whack. The shuttlecock is not so much launched as massaged by the catgut. She continues, laughs it off, but she cannot get the shuttlecock to cross the net. The sky is a bowl of darkest mussel-blue. Then rain. She runs inside. I hear music: Joy Division, 'Dead Souls'. The curtains are drawn. I smell burning herbs, cannabis. She is in pain. I know what I must do. I walk to Inshaw's. He offers to sail the boat for me, but I assure him I am a seasoned navigator. It is untrue. My upbringing proves fruitful for something: Inshaw lends me his boat for the day.

Miranda and I sail on the silver lake. The day turns bright and humid; a heron wades through the dark-green mud of the bank, water lilies spin with the current. The motor is off and I oar through syrupy, calm conditions till we come to the bend, continuing through a wider, willow-lined stretch, still on the estate. Here the wild flowers are in bloom, the eglantine, meadowsweet, great burnet. Low clouds of red admirals skim the water alongside the boat, their fat gravid centres like wet fur. In fields, I see bales of hay, barley being harvested. Her face has tilted to one side. Her freckled, yellowing face is beginning to develop a pronounced drop, with drooped jowls, and she drools when she speaks. In her eyes some recognition of what is happening to her. I will always be convinced by that look. I try to tip the boat. It is a struggle. The boat shudders, takes a while to capsize. She screams, splashes about. I swim towards her, hold her, our bodies small and snug in the water. My plan is to swim back once she has gone under, but I can't leave. She clings to me, accepting and placid.

Twenty-four hours later, I wash up against a bank. I am alive, and later wake up in hospital. Miranda floats to an island in the river, into a swan's nest. She is so white, two diving teams fail to spot her, wound around the reeds and tall red crocus.

Twenty-two summers pass. The world is a changed place.

Redwood belongs now to Inshaw. He grants me a walk through the estate whenever I come here. Around the mile or so of angular hedges, the ancient oak and badminton court, where, sometimes, I think I hear the wind fluting through plastic.

Once he asked if I was happy. Before I had the chance to reply, he said his own life had been good and prosperous, but hardly happy. Mine was the same, I said. What is happiness? he asked, as if I knew any better than he. I pondered on this. For me, I said, happiness is two girls playing badminton under an azure sky with clouds that are bird-shaped. Those summers were best, he replied, when I used to watch you play. It occurred to me then, that for nearly a quarter of a century we had both been sustained by a few intoxicating memories squirrelled from our youth. I told him it was high time we lived a little. He agreed and told me then of his plans to flatten the court. I remember that as I walked towards my car, parked beside the silver lake, I had the distinct and certain feeling I was being watched.

# THE WOMEN WRITERS' HANDBOOK

## Jaki McCarrick

McCarrick is an award-winning writer of plays, poetry and fiction. She won the 2010 Papatango New Writing Prize for her play *Leopoldville*, and her play *Belfast Girls*, developed at the National Theatre London, was shortlisted for the Susan Smith Blackburn Prize and the 2014 BBC Tony Doyle Award. *Belfast Girls* premiered in Chicago in May 2015 to much critical acclaim (Windy City Times Critics' Pick) and was staged in Canada and Australia. She has also recently been selected for the Irish Film Board's Talent Development Initiative to adapt *Belfast Girls* for the screen. Her play *The Naturalists* (Aurora Metro Books) premiered in New York in 2018.

> *"Controversy is part of the nature of art and creativity."*
> — Yoko Ono

# INTERVIEW WITH LAURA MILES

**Q. What drove you to write** *Transgender Resistance* **now?**
A. There were several reasons. Partly it was to offer a brief history of trans oppression and the roots of that oppression in class societies, in particular capitalism, from an explicitly socialist, historical materialist perspective. There is quite a lot of material around on sexual orientation and homophobia in class societies, for example by Jeffrey Weeks, and a good deal on Marxism and women's liberation, such as Judith Orr's book from 2015, but there's very little to date that seeks to apply a Marxist analysis to trans lives and experiences. Books by trans people, with a few exceptions, tend to be either autobiographies or are written from non-Marxist perspectives so I wanted to address the issues very differently.

I also wanted to present a picture of trans lives and experiences not just in Britain but internationally. That picture is varied but allows us to appreciate the high levels of transphobia that trans people have to contend with, but also the many ways in which they organise to resist and fight back.

I particularly wanted to engage with the current situation around updating the Gender Recognition Act. Since I began writing the book several years ago this has become a much more prominent issue in the press and on social media, in trade unions and political parties. There has been an enormous and often vitriolic backlash to some very modest proposals to update the Act, proposals such as self-declaration to obtain a Gender Recognition Certificate which have been implemented in various other countries with no ill effects. The backlash has led the UK and Scottish governments to delay the changes. People should realise that the cost of this is being paid for in trans people's health, lives and wellbeing.

## WOMEN'S VOICES

I have particularly addressed the "clash of women's and trans rights" narrative being deployed by some radical feminist and socialist opponents of the proposed reforms. Because I believe the starting point for any socialist should be unconditional support for oppressed people, it's very disappointing that a few people on the left and some radical feminists are using biological essentialist arguments to oppose the amendments.

They claim that science is on their side but they're wrong. There was a very good article in *The Lancet* recently by Katrina Karkazis ("The misuses of 'biological sex'", 23 November 2019), unfortunately published too late to be referenced in my book. The author shows how rigidly using discrete biological criteria to determine sex is misused for socio-political purposes, to include or exclude certain people from social categories that can access (or not) rights, services and so on. It is clear to me that the aim of the transphobes and trans critics, on the basis of scaremongering with little or no evidence, is to exclude trans people, particularly trans women, from single-sex spaces such as public toilets and to deny equal rights to an oppressed minority.

I have engaged with these "gender-critical" or "trans-critical" arguments in the book to demonstrate how regressive, damaging and poorly thought through they are. What we need is unity in action, not division, involving women, trans people and others to resist the austerity hitting women and trans people. We will need it more than ever as the nightmare reality of Johnson's Tory government unfolds, especially with the threat of another economic recession down the road.

**Q. Could you say something about your own history and experience of transitioning?**

A. There were few, if any, role models for gender variant people when I was younger and the general social atmosphere towards LGBT+ people was hostile, salacious and dangerously misinformed. Hats off to those brave people who fought back against huge odds. Not until Stonewall in 1969, did a movement emerge that asserted pride in being LGBT+ and demanded rights and respect. We need that sort of gutsiness and public protest again!

## THE WOMEN WRITERS' HANDBOOK

I first came out publicly at a NATFHE union conference in the early noughties speaking in a debate on gay and trans rights. I felt I needed to be honest about myself if I was to argue for unity of LGBT+ people.

Things progressed quite quickly after that. I became active in trade union equality forums and a few years later was elected as an LGBT rep on the University and College Union's national executive committee, a positon I held until 2015. I think I was the first openly trans person elected to the executive of a British trade union.

In 2010 I decided to transition to living full time as Laura. I was luckier than many trans people in that I was able to do this while keeping my lecturing job at Bradford College. I will always be thankful for the support of my partner, Sheila, my family, my union, and my comrades in the Socialist Workers Party and beyond. Apart from one or two negative instances, colleagues at work and my students were brilliantly supportive. Often curious, but brilliantly supportive!

**Q.You cover a lot of history in the book. Why is this important to you?**

A. Partly it was to demonstrate that transgender people have been around for a very long time in every society and that different, non-binary gender expression is a natural part of humanity just as different sexualities are. Some societies have not only tolerated gender variant individuals but have celebrated them, in stark contrast to modern capitalist societies where transphobia has at times been absolutely deadly and is currently being ramped up by the alt-right and far-right.

I wanted to show that just as the rise of class societies and the exploitation and expropriation at the heart of these led to the systematic oppression and dispossession of women, as Engels described in *The Origin of the Family, Private Property and the State*, the oppression of women rooted in the family also led to the oppression of alternative sexualities and gender expressions.

There is also a long history of resistance to these oppressions, including resistance to transphobia. The most far-reaching was the Stonewall Riot, a rebellion involving gays, lesbians and many trans people such as Sylvia Rivera and her friend Marsha P. Johnson, in 1969. Unfortunately trans people were increasingly relegated to the back of the bus when it came to the subsequent fight for better rights and were even excluded from some Pride marches. We have had to fight hard over the decades since then to be heard.

I was also very keen to explore the links between socialist individuals and organisations and the fight for LGBT+ rights. Prior to the Great War these links were explicit, the best example being the Bolshevik Party in Russia, which quickly decriminalised gay sex after the 1917 revolution, among many other progressive social measures. That link was broken by the rise of the Nazis in Germany, the concentration camps, and Stalinism in Russia.

The history of the left and the history of the struggle for LGBT+ rights are intimately linked. Periods of greatest advances for LGBT+ rights have generally been associated with periods of major advance for the working class, internationally and in particular nation states. The Russian Revolution is the prime example of this.

Conversely, periods of retreat and mortal danger for LGBT+ people have been those times when the working class and the left have suffered their greatest defeats. The 1930s and the rise of the Nazis is the most obvious example. There are huge lessons for us to learn in this.

Much of the international left after the Second World War, influenced by Stalinism, retained a view of homosexuality and gender variance as "bourgeois deviations" and any fight against LGBT+phobia and oppression was seen as a diversion from the class struggle.

In the 1970s elements of the New Left challenged this regressive orthodoxy, including the Socialist Workers Party, some of whose activists were prominent in the fight for gay rights in unions and workplaces. It took a great deal of agitation to ensure that the trade union movement in Britain took LGBT+ rights seriously but today most unions actively campaign for these and, not incidentally, support amendments to the GRA (Gender Recognition Act).

**Q. There are substantial sections on gender and gender identity. How much does having a clear understanding of these issues help us to build effective resistance to transphobia?**

## THE WOMEN WRITERS' HANDBOOK

A. I think it's essential. Since the late 1970s, at least, Marxist explanations of oppression were eclipsed by postmodern approaches which downplayed class and class struggle. This was a reflection of the general decline in levels of class struggle, the rise of neoliberalism and the dominance of identity politics which sees individual differences and categories of oppression as more fundamental than social class and class struggle.

I'd suggest that today most young LGBT+ activists are influenced by intersectionality and privilege theory. I have spent some time in the book examining the origins, strengths and weaknesses of these approaches. I wanted to make the point that when it comes to fighting oppression we can and should be fighting shoulder to shoulder, but obviously the theoretical views that a person holds are going to influence who they think is the main enemy, how we should fight back, and whether that can be alongside others in united fronts or autonomously.

In some ways thinking intersectionally about oppression is a step forward from previous identity theories in that it recognises particular oppressions cannot be dealt with in isolation. Most anti-racists, feminists and LGBT+ activists who look to intersectional theory in practice embrace trans rights and are not exclusionary towards trans people.

Where I think the approach is fundamentally weak, however, is that it doesn't recognise that the roots of oppression lie in the exploitative nature of capitalism. Marxists argue that class is much more than an "also ran" form of domination: it is fundamental to the social relations of production and reproduction in capitalism. Consequently we have to look to class struggle at the point of production, where the system's profits and lifeblood can be squeezed, as well as struggles against oppression per se, as the means to win our liberation.

**Q. What did you learn in the process of researching and writing this book?**

A. I found it a hugely educative experience. I was left with the most enormous respect and admiration for the generations of LGBT+ activists, especially trans activists, who have fought to be able to express their gender identity and sexuality often in the most difficult and dire circumstances, and to organise collectively. Many paid with their lives and liberty, and of course they still do in many countries.

Being LGB or trans remains illegal in many countries, but even in Western countries with more liberal social legislation levels of transphobia remain high and are being ramped up. The recent Tory victory bodes ill for all sorts of marginalised and vulnerable groups including trans people unless we can build much greater resistance in our communities, on the streets and in our workplaces.

**Q. Who do you hope will read it?**

A. I didn't set out to write an academic book but on the other hand I knew that for maximum clarity of politics and purpose it needed to address some of the theoretical arguments. I wrote it for trans people themselves, especially trans activists, about our history and struggles, but also for socialists in general and all those who have questions about trans lives and gender identity. It's therefore also intended for the many cisgender or non-trans people who support and want to fight alongside trans people in their struggle for transgender liberation. I hope that trans people and other readers will agree that liberation for trans people and all the oppressed will require revolutionary struggle to overthrow capitalism and create socialist societies.

*This interview is included with permission from The Socialist Review.*

**Laura Miles**

Laura is the author of *Transgender Resistance: Socialism and the Fight for Trans Liberation*, (Bookmarks). She was a lecturer at Bradford College and a leading member of the lecturers' unions NATFHE and UCU.

# THE MOTHERLOAD

## Raman Mundair

"The pram in the hall" has always been seen as a slamming of brakes on creativity. Some writers have often gone out of their way to avoid the responsibilities of parenthood. But for those of us who choose parenthood, it doesn't have to be a full stop, or even a comma, in our creativity.

Now let me clarify from the outset, I am not of the opinion that a woman needs to be a mother or choose parenthood in order to be complete. It is a choice or a circumstance that simply isn't for everyone. But here, now, I write in celebration of being a parent, a mother and a writer and artist.

I am a writer (and artist) mother to three young children under five. This means I have to be inventive and careful with my time and energy. I find that my practice has transformed. I am more effective with my time. There is less preamble. I have dispensed with many of my pre-motherhood writer rituals – for example, the endless cups of coffee, the preparing of space, the hours lost to "research" that may in actuality have no bearing on the work. No. All of that has gone.

The lead into work has taken on a different form. I create in a different way. I have developed a new, effective methodology which offers me maximum output from the limited time and energy I have. My approach to research has changed. Everything I undertake has to balance with Parent/Motherhood. My time is valuable. Precious. I choose. I choose carefully. I choose carefully what I do/make/act upon.

## WOMEN'S VOICES

I make work in a patchwork sort of fashion now. I "quilt" work from small, finite pieces of time, energy, that together offer a whole that will develop into a larger-scale idea. I find the process magnifies my material. I am close up, eye to eye with it for an intense moment and then move away. A forced distance (when practical motherhood activities beckon) allows an important time to process and reconfigure perspectives and ideas. When I return to the work, to the creating and making, I come with a new gaze and a new way of seeing that makes the work precise and full of rigour. I find it satisfying to work in this way.

My practice has also become more nocturnal. I often undertake "amritvela" work – amritvela is, in Hindu and Sikh culture, the sacred, silent dawn time of day. A time where everything is pregnant with possibility. When, if I have worked long into the night, a visceral exhaustion leaves me tender and vulnerable, but at the same time offers me clear sight. A raw, spiritual type of energy that has translated into fine work.

I am a mother, I am multitudes. I am a writer, I am multitudes.

When you are a parent/mother you are multitudes. When you are a writer and artist you are multitudes. I give my work and practice worth and demonstrate the importance of this to my kids. I give my practice status, that it is "work" and model that for my kids. So that my work is as important in their minds as something easily tangible such as a teacher or firefighter etc.

Being a writer and artist makes me feel like a better person and therefore a better mother. I mean this in the sense that I am at my best when I am making work, when my creativity is active and utilized. My children benefit from seeing their mother in her multitudes and with her creativity vital and in full flow.

I do not wish to end up at the end of my kids' childhood tremendously successful as a writer and artist but realizing that I do not really know my children – that I have no idea of who they really are. I don't want commercial/traditional success by any means necessary. Not at the cost of my relationship with my kids. Creative endeavours are impacted by intersectionality, for me, being a woman of colour, a working-class woman, a woman with a disability, a Queer woman, and being a Mother is all part

## THE WOMEN WRITERS' HANDBOOK

of the intersections that I have to navigate to get to the work. Managing to be creative at the same time as raising children is a revolutionary act. Parenthood demands sacrifice. Complete submission at times. To find a pocket of air within that for writing, creative work, dialogue or practice is an extraordinary thing. Don't fear that pram in the hall! Rest assured, it can and will be done.

**Raman Mundair**

Raman is an Indian-born, Queer, British Asian intersectional feminist and activist based in Shetland and Glasgow. She is the award-winning author of *Lovers, Liars, Conjurers and Thieves*, *A Choreographer's Cartography*, *The Algebra of Freedom*, a play, (Aurora Metro Books) and is the editor of *Incoming: Some Shetland Voices*. As an activist she has worked at a grassroots level against racism, fascism, state violence, and against gender-based, domestic and sexual violence. www.shetlandamenity.org/the-artist

Woodcut by Julie de Graag

# THE FEMINIST LIBRARY

## Magda Oldziejewska

Being a writer is not something I dreamed about when I was a child. I did write diaries – I went through many in my teenage years – but it just wasn't on my dream list of professional pursuits. Not until I became a feminist and joined the Feminist Library collective anyway, and even then, it happened somewhat accidentally, one might say. Now it seems like it should have been an obvious choice.

The Feminist Library is an amazing place in London which collects and safeguards women's histories. It holds about 20,000 books and periodicals, plus archives, zines, pamphlets and countless ephemeral material... the list goes on. But that's not all. Perhaps most crucially, personally at least, it is a place of community – a space where feminists gather, discuss, organize and create, together. And that last part is what's central to my story.

When I joined the Feminist Library I was at a crossroads – I had just quit my cushy, well-paid office job, that I hated, and decided to become a full-time feminist. I did not have much of a plan of how to go about making this happen. But it is now a reality – in no small part thanks to the Library, where I found my community, my calling and my niche. Today, one of the main, and my favourite, things to occupy my time with, is talking and writing about the Library, feminist spaces and herstory. None of this would have happened without the existence of a space like the Library.

And perhaps most importantly, I found empowerment in the true sense of this word, at the Library – I now truly believe that I can do just about anything. Trust me when I say that I did not grow up thinking that... But during my time at the Library, I have run fundraising, helped save the organization from closure, set up events programmes, helped run others, learned to speak publicly without fear and, most importantly, became a writer. Somewhat accidentally perhaps, but now it feels like that's exactly what I should be doing.

I say accidentally because it wasn't something that was on my agenda when I quit my job (or, indeed, before). Setting up a feminist café was, having more time for activism definitely was, but not writing. And then I realized, as I was working at the Library and going about my transition into full-time feminism, just how quickly we can lose our own herstory if we're not careful. Explorations in my "everyday feminism" journey – in writing, first in a diary form, eventually transferred onto a blog, then several, as well as articles in other publications, conference papers and presentations – became an integral part of it. And now I have something to share with young feminists who want to go down the same path but don't really know how to go about it. As well as dozens of other stories – I now write about forgotten women's histories, feminist spaces, Polish feminism and more! Working at the Library has opened up new directions for me, including ones I'd never even thought of before. I gradually started speaking publicly, more recently at academic conferences, which helped develop my confidence. And I have just applied to do a PhD on the Library's herstory and organisation as a result of one of these talks!

I honestly have no idea where I would have been today if it wasn't for the Feminist Library. All I hope for the Library is that it remains in existence long into the future, so that all women who need it can find it and make the most of it too. It truly is an inspirational and unique space, in more ways than one. And I am blessed to call it my second home, a space of feminist sisterhood, a room of my own – with enough herstory to inspire a lifetime. Virginia Woolf would have loved it.

Following a successful Crowdfunding campaign, where we were able to go beyond our initial target, we have recently moved to a new space at The Sojourner Truth Community Centre, 161 Sumner Rd, Peckham, London SE15 6JL.

*Why not come and visit and say hello or join us as a volunteer?*

# WOMEN'S VOICES

## Magda Oldziejewska

Magda Oldziejewska is a Polish feminist activist, organiser, writer and researcher. She is currently a member of the Feminist Library management collective, as well as its Fundraising Coordinator. She has founded several feminist organisations, including, most recently, FARSA – feminist artivists – a Polish feminist organisation in London, promoting feminism through art, with a focus on reproductive rights.

# FORTUNE FAVOURS THE BRAVE, BUT CHANCE FAVOURS THE PREPARED MIND

## Kaite O'Reilly

Maybe it's my greed for experience, but I have always wanted to lead several lives, a desire made manifest through my choice of projects and parallel careers. I have been a physical theatre performer, a chambermaid, a live art practitioner and a relief aid worker in war zones. I have written libretti, radio drama, short film, prose; sold shoes, meat and copy; directed film and dance theatre; been a writer-in-residence and Creative Fellow and supervised postgraduate degrees in writing for performance whilst participating in Deaf arts, disability culture and the so-called mainstream.

I think one of the most important lessons I have learnt is never to perceive myself as one thing. This business will often try to label us, slap a convenient sticker on our forehead and file us away under a limiting, narrow definition. Although often seen as perverse, I pride myself on not being easy to define. I try to keep experimenting, taking on new challenges and developing my skills. I've often found in the UK that diversity is seen as an anomaly, a vulgar excess to be treated with suspicion. Phrases like "jack of all trades, master of none" damn the Renaissance wo/man. I know writers who have limited their careers and creativity by believing it's inappropriate to try something new, or that there are set patterns and processes to adhere to (if only they could decipher them), rather than inventing new ones.

## WOMEN'S VOICES

But it's difficult and daunting to initiate projects and career paths, especially when writers are often solitary figures in an industry that seems to work in mysterious ways. How to progress is a central question. I spent years expecting everything to suddenly become clear once I had gained enough experience, but now I don't believe there is one route, method or direction. This is a territory that can't be definitively mapped. Yet when I look back over my own career, there is a logical pattern, an apparently designed trajectory, although my progress felt haphazard and peripatetic at the time. The only conclusion I can draw is the importance of being guided through the labyrinth by individual curiosity and passions. It is the only way to stop getting "lost" or losing time in dead-end pursuits.

Too often, emerging writers second-guess what directors or publishers want, or copy trends rather than setting them, or enter into a strange ventriloquism using a borrowed voice, not their own. When developing new writers, I encourage them to work from their passion/s, to identify and locate what engages or fascinates them. I've found that this engagement will often translate into the quality of the work, providing the writer with their particular viewpoint, whilst sustaining them through the long and often arduous process of rewriting. When writers are truly connected to their material they are unlikely to abandon the project – and I think it essential to finish things – their practice is often richer and more complex and they're less willing to accept second best. It also means the work has content – the writers have something to communicate.

When I started out as a playwright, it was still usual to send one copy of the script out at a time and then endure an agonizing wait of many months to hear from the agent/literary manager/editor/director, only to repeat the hateful pattern all over again. I learnt to cultivate a third skin (a second isn't thick enough) and, despite my sympathies for the invariably over-worked literary gatekeeper, to loathe the power balance. I wanted to be in control as much as I could be of my life, my work and any emerging neuroses. The depressive, solitary writer waiting anxiously by the letterbox was all too possible, so I distracted myself by reading widely and hungrily the work of women writers in other countries and centuries and exploring performance aesthetics which had fired my imagination.

## THE WOMEN WRITERS' HANDBOOK

My understanding of dramaturgy and the multiplicity of theatre languages bloomed when I became increasingly involved in disability arts and culture and collaborating with deaf practitioners, using visual language in performance alongside spoken and projected English. A new horizon of performative and dramaturgical possibilities opened before me, along with new markets and opportunities outside the UK. Without realizing it, I had embarked on my freelance career and begun my own professional development. By following my curiosity and being open to new experiences, writing, and form, I grew – and by developing further skills in application writing and producing, I became increasingly in control. I was no longer the passive female writer and maker, but one who was pro-active, controlling and owning "the means of production".

But writers are often shy creatures, backstage, off-camera. It is asking a lot to expect them to be suddenly dynamic and inventive, which is where networks or informal support systems come into their own. I have a close group of allies and friends who act as sounding boards, dramaturgs, editors and actors for readings of works-in-progress. We barter and pool our skills, mentoring and nurturing one another. When starting out, we even impersonated each other to bypass nerves or modesty, finding it easier to chase up one another's contacts and scripts rather than our own. Being part of a community is invaluable, as is learning to collaborate and ask for help. I think being aware of our fascinations is important – being alert and conscious of what fires our imagination – and ready to act on it.

Fortune may favour the brave, but as Louis Pasteur advised: chance favours the prepared mind.

*Extracted from 'How Did I Get Here?' The Writer's Compass. National Association of Writers in Education. https://www.nawe.co.uk*

# WOMEN'S VOICES

## Kaite O'Reilly

Kaite O'Reilly is a playwright, radio dramatist, writer, and dramaturg who works in disability arts and culture and mainstream culture. She has won many awards for her work, including the Peggy Ramsay Award for *Yard* (The Bush, London), Manchester Theatre Award's best play of the year for *Perfect* (Contact Theatre), Theatre-Wales Award for *peeling* (Graeae Theatre company) published by Aurora Metro Books, and the Ted Hughes Award for Poetry for her reworking of Aeschylus's *Persians* for National Theatre Wales in their inaugural year. She was a finalist in the Susan Smith Blackburn Prize for her play about memory and brain injury *The Almond and the Seahorse* and honoured in the 2018 Elliot Hayes for Outstanding Achievement in Dramaturgy for *And Suddenly I Disappear: The Singapore/UK 'd' Monologues*. Widely published and produced, she works internationally, with plays translated/produced in 11 countries worldwide.

# INTERVIEW WITH JACQUELINE PEPALL

**Q. What aspects of life and, and particularly women's lives do you think need more representation on screen?**

A. I had this epiphany a couple of years ago, because I think when we're growing up, we just consume film and TV and we don't question it, or at least I didn't. The women I was seeing onscreen twenty years ago were very singular in the way they were represented. It didn't occur to me that I was only seeing one aspect of the female teenage experience, about clothes and relationships. And there was nothing else. I never saw a female story that reflected my actual experience, and it wasn't until I was older that I realized these stories I was watching were always told by male writers and male directors – and that it was middle aged men who decided what the female teenage experience looked and felt like.

And we didn't really vary from that until recently, with films like *Lady Bird* and *Booksmart* giving a much broader and more accurate representation of female stories, especially teenage female stories. Simultaneously I also came to the realization that when I was younger, because I grew up with a brother, we would watch a lot of action films. And I never wanted to be the female character. I never wanted to be Sandra Bullock in *Speed*. I wanted to be Keanu Reeves in *Speed*. And it occurred to me that I was inventing these characters when I was 10, and I would imagine myself in these roles and invent this completely different woman that would be the main character of the film and the hero – instead of just the love interest. And it wasn't until I was in my late twenties and actively making TV that it occurred to me that I grew up on this diet of really badly portrayed

## WOMEN'S VOICES

female characters. At that point I felt like the whole purpose of my career was to give young women the heroes that I didn't have growing up.

**Q. Could you tell me a little bit more about what a screen lab involves and how it can help you in your career?**

A. The process of making something for the screen is very collaborative and you're working with a big team, but often when you're getting projects off the ground, it's very isolating. I recently finished the Edinburgh Talent Lab, and just being with 29 other people that were doing the same thing and on that same journey was so valuable. And I think sometimes we forget how isolated we are because we're so focused on getting this project up and running or meeting this deadline, and we forget that there are lots of other people out there going through exactly the same thing.

So for me, it's all about the people that you meet on labs and the relationships that you make. I made so many friends on the Edinburgh Lab who were at exactly my level in the film industry – and across different roles, too, because the Edinburgh Lab had a lot of producers. Before that experience I had a couple of producers that I worked with, now I know fifteen that I really like and want to work with. So for me, because I'm not a great networker, I find those things really tricky and challenging, but when you're on a lab with other people, then it's an inbuilt friendship because you're all there together. You're out of your life for a couple of days. And I think that's just such a lovely, valuable experience.

**Q. Could you tell me a little bit about the positives and perhaps the challenges of directing your own writing?**

A. I think one of the positive things for me is that when I'm directing something that I've written, I've completely visualized it. So I'm not starting from scratch. It's not the same if I'm directing something that someone else has written. Even though when I read the script, I see glimpses of the film, I see what it's going to be, it's not quite as vivid.

I also think sometimes when you're directing something that you've written, if you painted yourself into a corner with the writing – you can't blame the writer, you are the writer. You have to deal with it, which I think is a good thing. Conversely, I think sometimes the negative is that if something comes up on set and it really needs to be changed, or something's not working for an actor, at that point when I'm directing, my writing brain is completely turned off. I almost need someone else to tell me how to fix that. I think it's different for everybody. I know there are writers and directors that can go away for a few minutes and rewrite the scene and come back. And I think when you're directing there are lots of times when you're behind or you worry that you're not getting the right stuff, or you're just worried that you're not doing a good enough job. And then I think that can sometimes be compounded if you've also written the material.

I was shooting a film a couple of months ago in Chile and we were really behind. I was directing it and I had written it and I had this moment where I just kind of stepped away for a minute, trying to regain my thoughts and thinking – I've got to right the ship. But then I also had a crisis of confidence about 'who wrote this?' You're always going to have a bit of a crisis of confidence in any creative project, directing or writing. And it's kind of unfortunate when the two come at once.

**Q. Have you ever experienced your writing being directed by somebody else?**

A. I haven't actually. I'm not necessarily opposed to that, but I haven't.

**Q. Could you tell me about the Wilderness Festival?**

A. The Hospital Club in London has a programme for emerging creatives across all disciplines. In 2017, I was their film emerging creative, which means that they give you a membership to the club and you have access to the screening room and the facilities and they promote your work. I was coming to the end of my year as an emerging creative and I'd had screenings of my work and I'd had events that were about me as a filmmaker. And I felt because my time there was coming to an end, I needed to do something that wasn't just about me. And at the same time I had a lot of friends who had films that just didn't hit the right notes to get into the right festivals – but the films are still great. And I just felt like I could use the resources that I had to support other female filmmakers and give people a platform to show their work for free.

And I didn't know if people would be interested. I didn't know if anyone would come, but I thought at the very least, I'll run three days

## WOMEN'S VOICES

of short films by female filmmakers. You don't have to pay to come to the event and you don't have to pay to submit your film. Basically we're just giving female filmmakers a platform to share their work with a wider audience. And what was amazing was that we just completely packed the house every time. We even got in trouble because we had people sitting in the aisles because we were over capacity.

It was wonderful. I was just so happy that people were interested. And then we did it again the next year. I wondered if we could do it again? Did we hit a nerve in 2017? But exactly the same thing happened. There was even a big snow storm on one of the nights, and we still had a packed house. And so it just felt like there was this huge appetite to come see short films by female filmmakers that we didn't know existed.

**Q. That's fantastic. Is it going to continue?**

A. I didn't manage to get it off the ground this year because they were in transition between two different people. But we'll keep it going.

**Q. Is there a really good decision that you made in your career? And also perhaps a decision that you regret?**

A. I started directing first, and came to writing later. I think I just had no confidence as a writer. I didn't think that I could do it. I always felt like I was meant to direct, but I felt like writing my own work wasn't something that I would ever be able to do. I can't remember what happened or what shifted but I just started writing a short film just to see if I could do it. And something that was really key for me was writing it by hand. Something about being at a computer and working on the script software made everything that I wrote feel too final. If I could start writing the film by hand, the ideas would come quicker.

I wasn't as censored and so to be honest, the best creative decision that I've made was to just try writing. Because it turned out that it was this incredibly joyful thing for me. And in order to direct, you need money and you need a team and you need all this stuff in order to be creative. Whereas writing was a way for me to be creative between directing projects, and I just needed myself and some time and I could do it. So definitely, and it's only been two years that I've been actively also a screenwriter. All I needed to do was take that plunge.

## THE WOMEN WRITERS' HANDBOOK

And I think a decision that I regret, in my early years as a director, was my eagerness – I would direct anything. So I worked on a natural history series. I worked on a dance series. I would work on any factual series, anything that would allow me to get behind the camera, which I think is probably a good approach. But what happened is the film and TV industry just want to pigeonhole you. Are you a comedy director? Are you a drama director? Are you a natural history director?

You have to pick. And because I did a bit of everything early on, I found that a couple of years into my career, I had to make a conscious choice about what it was that I wanted to do and only do that thing. In my case, scripted comedy and drama. I sometimes wonder, because I'd always known that that was what I wanted to do, if I'd been a little bit more focused from the beginning, if I would have gotten places quicker.

**Q. Are there any female writers or filmmakers that you really admire and that have inspired you?**

A. Well, there's Phoebe Waller-Bridge's *Fleabag* of course. And Sharon Horgan is incredible too. I can't get enough of what they do. They're both so incredibly prolific. And the quality is amazing. And those two would definitely be role models for me.

**Q. How much of your own experience informs your writing?**

A. I would say quite a bit. I think I don't always necessarily write about things that are directly related to my life, but there's always an emotional connection to my direct experience.

**Q. And what do you think of the argument that writers should only write based on their own experience or their own cultural background?**

A. I think as long as you can get emotional truth right then you can write it. I mean certainly there's a lot of times when it's inappropriate to write about something that's not your own experience, but I think broadly speaking to tell the writer that they should only write from their lived experience is so limiting. Because if we did that, we wouldn't have any fantasy and science fiction. I had a really positive experience earlier this year when I was hired to write a film for a Chilean actress and I don't speak

Spanish. I've never been to Chile. But we were friends and I felt like I could tap into what she wanted to achieve, and the film that she wanted to make.

I wrote a mother/daughter story that was loosely based on my own experiences. What was so interesting was that even though the kind of cultural language needed to be tweaked, the emotional truth of the mother/daughter relationship was exactly the same for all the Chilean women that worked on the film.

**Q. What are you most proud of in your career?**

A. That's a tricky one. Actually, I think at the moment, the piece of work that I really like is the Chilean film that I just finished. But I also think that writing and directing and just sort of being in a creative industry, you just have to suffer so much rejection, and keep getting back up. And sometimes I am grateful that I have gotten this far and I haven't given up because there were so many times when the road felt like, I can't do it anymore. I can't, I can't keep going down this path. And I'm proud that I got back up every time.

**Q. Do you think that technology has altered your practice in terms of how films are made and how they're consumed?**

A. I think technology's just made filmmaking so much more accessible. I can't imagine how hard it must've been for a filmmaker growing up in the 80s or the early 90s. Trying to get your films made because you needed these big editing systems and you needed a proper editor to cut the film.

With streaming platforms like Netflix and Amazon, a lot of filmmakers get stressed that we're moving away from cinema, from the big screen cinema experience – but I am happy that we're telling lots of stories and we're telling really different stories, and there seems to be this huge appetite for narrative storytelling. And I'm not so bothered about whether that's on a computer screen or a phone or a cinema screen. I'm happy that there are lots of places now that we can go to tell stories.

**Q. What's the best piece of professional advice you've been given?**

A. I think probably from a writing perspective you just have to start. I think it was Stephen Mangan who tweeted that you have to know that when you start writing it's going to be a bit crap and that's okay. I think that that really helped me because I really like Stephen Mangan and I like his writing. I think the idea that you're going to go through a phase where it's going to be bad and the point is, to stay with it through that phase and then you'll come out the other side.

It's really good advice for everything. That's good advice for directing. You know that when you're in the edit on a piece that you've directed, there's very much a cycle where you start off well and then it feels really terrible and you're never going to get out of it – and then it ends up pretty good again. I think it's just recognizing that that trajectory exists for all creative projects and you have to make it through the phase where it's not working and just keep going.

**Jacqueline Pepall**

Jacqueline Pepall is an award-winning writer/director for film and TV. She is currently directing 5 episodes of a teen comedy for Nickelodeon. As a writer, her work has been shortlisted for the Sundance Episodic Lab, 2019. Her feature film, *Goblin Market* is in formal development with the BFI. She has television projects in development with the BBC and Channel 4. Her short film credits include *Wishin' & Hopin'* (BFI Flare 2018), *The Hotel Affair* (London Short Film Festival 2018), and *Ophelia's End* (Best Film, Dallas Flicks by Chicks Film Festival 2017). She created and directed the contemporary dance series, *Then Dance* (Sky Arts) and the comedy pilot *Upstaged* (CBC Canada, winner: Best Pilot, LA Comedy Festival).

The UK Trade and Investment Commission recently selected Pepall for their "UK Talent Goes to Hollywood" initiative, which pairs promising British directors with Hollywood studios. She is part of the Edinburgh International Film Festival's 2019 Talent Lab. She is the recipient of a John Brabourne Award, Autumn 2019. She organizes and runs an annual film festival, "From the Wilderness", championing the work of female directors. Her work celebrates new, underrepresented heroes.

> *"Above all,
> be the heroine of your life,
> not the victim."*
> — Nora Ephron

# ON TRANSLATION, NABOKOV AND KNITTING

## Gabi Reigh

When the first novel I translated, *The Town with Acacia Trees* by Mihail Sebastian, was published, I posted a picture of it on Facebook and announced that I was taking a break from knitting things nobody wants to translating books nobody reads. It was not intended as a commentary on the quality of the book, but a nod to the relative invisibility of literature in translation in the UK, where despite recent growth, it still only accounts for around 6% of all published fiction.

Despite the Sisyphean task of persuading the public (and publishers) to take an interest in the international literary gems buried in their laptops, translators persevere because they see themselves as intercessors between cultures, impelled by a noble calling to bring into being books that will allow readers to 'slip into the soul' of someone on the other side of the world. What's more, they see themselves as artists, rallying around the hashtag #NameTheTranslator, decrying the failure of newspapers or reviewers to credit their work or ignore the fact that they were responsible for shaping the beauty of the literary text.

Personally, I feel content in the shadows. If I read a review praising Sebastian's playful tone or lyrical imagery, I am mostly just relieved that I haven't spoiled his novel through my translation. To some extent, the translators' insistence on being given the status of artists could be understood as a reaction against the sniping that they are regularly

## WOMEN'S VOICES

subjected to. On a literary translation forum, one translator announced that his New Year's resolution was to tackle anyone who uses the phrase 'lost in translation.' For every person who extols the virtues of reading international literature, there is an army who will argue that there is something not quite genuine about these works, that their meaning has been diluted by being transmuted into a different language.

Reading Vladimir Nabokov's *The Art of Translation – the sins of translation and the Russian short story*, I'm struck by a sense of foreboding from the very first sentence:

"Three grades of evil can be discerned in the queer world of verbal transmigration."

I read on, preparing myself to be chastised by one of my favourite writers, and he does not disappoint. The mortal sins that a translator might be guilty of are: a poor command of the original language, skipping passages that he/she is too lazy/stupid to comprehend and "the third, and worst, degree of turpitude is reached when a masterpiece is planished and patted into such a shape, vilely beautified in such a fashion as to conform to the notions and prejudices of a given public." Reading such translations, Nabokov complains, leave him "with the impression that [he is] witnessing a murder and can do nothing to prevent it."

There is no denying the fact that there is something slippery about literary translation. Nabokov knew it too. For as much as he denounced those who stray away from faithfully decoding the original text, he also admitted that such a literal version is likely to be an artistic failure:

"What is to be done with this bird you have shot down only to find that it is not a bird of paradise, but an escaped parrot, still screeching its idiotic message as it flaps on the ground?"

I confess that when I translate, I sometimes have the feeling that I'm committing some kind of fraud, as if I'm counterfeiting banknotes which I will try to palm off as genuine to an unsuspecting shopkeeper. It is because when I'm translating, I have to reinvent the voice behind the page, the voice I listen to carefully, sympathetically, but which I have to recreate using words which the writer did not even know existed. It is a form of ventriloquism, with me as the dummy through which the author speaks. Nabokov wrote that the ideal translator "must possess the gift of mimicry and be able to act, as it were, the real author's part by impersonating his tricks of demeanor and speech, his ways and his mind, with the utmost degree of verisimilitude."

But how can such verisimilitude be achieved when "the interrelation of words and non-correspondence of verbal series in different tongues" cause the translator to falter, to question which is the best way to deliver the words of the ventriloquist? The writer would have selected words and sentence structures which create certain resonances in the original language, strike invisible chords in the reader's imagination. Yet the same words, in the same order, can fall flat when translated into a new language.

I was asked once in an interview what menu I would cook at a dinner party for the interwar writers whose work I've translated. The answer I gave was just as bizarre as the question: I said that it would have to be some kind of literary feast comprised of French food mentioned in Sebastian's novel *Women*, followed by a traditional Romanian main like *sarmale* (cabbage rolls stuffed with mince), culminating in an English dessert like spotted dick and custard. I had to admit that while this menu, with its melding of different cultures, might be a fitting metaphor for the translation process, it would amount to a fairly indigestible meal. When creating a literary translation, you need to be aware of the differences between languages and understand that what works in one might sound dissonant in another. A translation must retain the emotional power of the original and become an independent work of art in itself, rather than trying to accommodate discordant elements which will make it sound just as unappealing as my imaginary dinner party menu.

Stephen Fry believes that "[English] certainly has the largest vocabulary … by a long, long, long long, way. Rather as China is to the rest of the world in population, English is in the population of its words." There are so many choices to be made as a translator, walking on the tightrope between faithfulness to the original and sensitive evocation of tone. When someone calls out as they stub their toe, is it a 'shout', or a 'shriek', or a 'cry', or a 'scream'? I have to decide. A translation is woven out of thousands of such tiny choices and in this way it becomes the brainchild of the translator as well as that of the original writer.

## WOMEN'S VOICES

So is this art? I see it more as craftsmanship, like building, or knitting, following a design laid out by somebody else, but creating something new nonetheless, something of your own. And why do it, if, more likely than not, readers will pick up a Scandinavian thriller rather than your Romanian interwar coming-of-age story? The only answer I have is that these books must exist. They must exist as a symbol that we still care enough to see through others' eyes, to 'slip into another's soul' even if we are separated by time and geography.

There are people living in the UK today who have left behind their own countries and embraced everything their new land has to offer, who read English books, watch English TV. These recent arrivals learn to understand their hosts, but their hosts are often blind to the cultures that have shaped their neighbours and fellow workers. The translator, working in the shadows, can introduce readers to literary classics from other countries, enabling greater understanding of those cultures and shining a light on the genius of foreign authors who would otherwise be little known.

### Gabi Reigh

Gabi Reigh was born in Romania and moved to the UK in her teens. She has won the Stephen Spender prize for poetry in translation and is currently engaged in a translation project called 'Interbellum Series' focusing on works from the Romanian interwar period. The first titles in this series were *Poems of Light* by Lucian Blaga and the novels *The Town with Acacia Trees* and *Women* by Mihail Sebastian (Aurora Metro). Sebastian's play *The Star with no Name* and Liviu Rebreanu's novel *Ciuleandra* will be published in 2020.

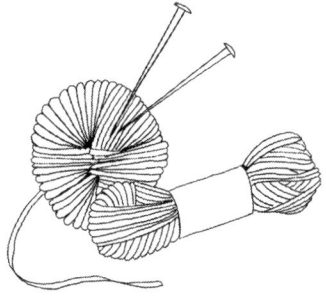

# CONSIDERATIONS OF AMEFRICANITY

## Djamila Ribeiro

"The risk we take here is that of speaking out with all its implications. Precisely because others have spoken for us, infantilized us (an infant is one who can't speak for herself, a child who speaks of herself in the third person, because adults speak on her behalf), so in this work we claim our own speech. In other words, the trash will talk, and it will be fine".[2]

This text begins with the words of Lélia Gonzalez (1935 – 1994), one of the great thinkers of Brazilian black feminism. A professor at the Pontifical Catholic University of Rio de Janeiro, Gonzalez, as we shall see, is the author of founding texts of concepts and perspectives of international feminist thought and has opened pathways for many of us in Brazil to follow in the dispute for our existence, knowledge and new possibilities. The contributions of black feminists as a whole have come to question man, both white and European, as the universal subject, as well as to question the universalization of the category of woman. If on the one hand, Simone de Beauvoir, in her work *The Second Sex*, when thinking about the condition of woman, defined her as being "the other" in relation to man, one who is not considered in her own right, but only as an adjunct of man, Grada Kilomba, an interdisciplinary thinker rooted in Germany, goes even further with the analysis to think of a black woman as

2 *Racism and Sexism in Brazilian Society*. In *Pensamento Feminista Brasileiro: formation and context* by Lélia Gonzalez. Rio de Janeiro: Bazar do Tempo, (2019).

## WOMEN'S VOICES

"the other of the other", since she is the double antithesis of both whiteness and masculinity. These differences in the starting point with regard to social position produce totally different perspectives and experiences in common with the group. In this sense, questioning the universalization of the category of woman, in *Blackening Feminism*, the Brazilian philosopher Sueli Carneiro, a memorable black feminist, asks the key question:

> "When we talk about the myth of women's fragility, which has historically justified men's paternalistic protection of women, which women are we talking about? We black women are part of a contingent of women, probably in the majority, who have never recognized this myth in themselves, because we have never been treated as fragile. We are part of a group of women who have worked for centuries as slaves on the plantations or on the streets, as saleswomen, greengrocers, prostitutes... Women who understood nothing when the feminists said that women should take over the streets and work! We are part of a group of women who are regarded as objects. Yesterday, in the service of frail little pimps and perverted, well-off lords. (...)
>
> Racism establishes the social inferiority of black segments of the population in general and of black women in particular, operating moreover as a factor of division in the struggle of women for the privileges that are instituted for white women. In this perspective, the fight of black women against the oppression of gender and race has been drawing new contours for feminist and anti-racist political action, enriching both the discussion of the racial question and the question of gender in Brazilian society.[3]"

Historically, movements of black men and women from different intellectual and political perspectives have worked to deconstruct the myth of racial democracy in the last Western country to abolish slavery in 1888. The abolition, merely formal, did not come with any public policy of integration into society, while the Brazilian state encouraged the arrival

---

3 *Blackening Feminism: The Situation of Black Women in Latin America from a Gender Perspective* by Sueli Carneiro. In *Pensamento Feminista Brasileiro: conceitos fundamentais*, org. Heloisa Buarque de Almeida. Rio de Janeiro: Bazar do Tempo.

of immigrants – Germans, Italians, Portuguese, among others – with the distribution of land and other affirmative policies. While the first Brazilian Constitution prohibited black people from studying, the country's Land Law conditioned the acquisition of land through purchase – with the exception of welcome immigrants, of course – as well as crimes which were created with the specific objective of imprisoning the unemployed for the crime of "loitering", affecting mainly black men, the Brazilian State officially instituted what was called a "whitening policy", aimed at erasing the black population that was associated with backwardness. The official whitening project included the forced sterilization of black women, a practice which was denounced in 1992 by the notable Parliamentary Commission of Inquiry of the Brazilian National Congress that was established after a broad struggle by the black women's movement in the 1980s. This commission concluded that, one hundred years after the formal end of slavery, black women in the North and Northeast, the most impoverished regions of the country, were still being sterilized without their knowledge.

Despite all the tricks and violence of the whitening project, the policy did not have the desired effect, since today 56% of the Brazilian population is black, being the largest black country outside of Africa. However, institutionalized racism has caused and continues to cause the abysmal difference between black and white people in terms of living conditions and opportunity.

According to Amnesty International data, every 23 minutes a young black man is murdered in Brazil. When they are not killed, these young people are imprisoned, making up more than two thirds of the 700,000 prisoners in the country. The intersections make the scenario even more complex in a country which is ranked 5th in the world for its child marriage and femicide.

In the last fifteen years, the imprisonment of women has increased by 567.4%, most of them black (68%) and mostly for drug trafficking (62%). In the field of work, women are an absolute minority in management positions, and when they occupy the same job as a man, they receive a lower salary. In the geography of the cities, the areas which are considered up-market are the white neighborhoods while the infamous "favelas" are inhabited mostly by black people.

Another harsh reality for the black population, is the stereotypical way that the Brazilian media monopolies belonging to white families, and composed mostly of white people, have historically passed off racial hatred in the form of humour and it is evidenced by the constant deprecation of black characters in comedies in order to make white people laugh.

On a visit to São Paulo, Angela Davis said that when she turned on Brazilian television, she thought she was in Finland, there was such a massive white representation in the media. Soap operas that take place in Bahia (a state where almost 90% of the population is black) employ only white actors, many of them from the Southeast who simply put on a Bahia accent. It is because of this widespread lack of representation for the black population, that studies claim that racial democracy in Brazil is a myth which is promulgated by the white elites to maintain their ongoing project of racial domination.

Under the current government, the data is even more worrying. The president's election was marked by hate speech towards minority populations and by the support of Christian religious groups, mainly neo-Pentecostal. Jair Bolsonaro had a clear run, when his opponent Lula was imprisoned on corruption and money laundering charges, upheld by judge Sergio Moro in a legal process that was contested worldwide. Who was surprised when Moro was later promoted to be the Minister for Justice in Bolsinaro's government? His election came after Dilma Rousseff, of the Workers' Party, resigned from the presidency, without having been convicted of any crime. Despite all the limitations, Dilma and Lula, both from the Workers' Party, had implemented important public policies to help people access higher education, benefiting the black population, something rare in the country's history and enough for them to be considered a major national nuisance.

In contrast to what had been achieved, the current government is undoing the good work of its predecessors and is bringing in new measures, such as imposing austerity reforms for the population, as well as labour and social security legislation which would be unthinkable in countries of the global North. It goes without saying that these reforms disproportionately affect the black and indigenous people in the country. This is an ongoing project of regression and neo-colonization. In Europe, leaders and "enlightened" people are often horrified, openly condemning what is happening in Brazilian politics. Although it is shocking to see the Amazon on fire, I think that if they knew about the policies being implemented for the black and indigenous communities, their shock would be even greater. The governor of Rio de Janeiro, for example, in the president's base, was elected by saying on stage that the police would "aim at the head" and shoot young people from dangerous communities. He has kept his promise. I understand that this shocks anyone with humanity, but it is worth saying that the neoliberal project that is underway in the country has put up for sale Brazilian state-owned aviation, oil wells, airports, energy companies, mining, among many other assets that are being privatized. And who is buying? Precisely those consortiums, multinationals, state companies and other organizations backed by capital from the global North, the same parties that clash with the current president on one side but happily fill the government's pockets through their sell-off of state assets on the other. Are those "enlightened" Europeans outraged by this too?

I once went to Berlin to attend the Book Fair. The invitation was to participate in a panel discussion that would explore issues under the current government in Brazil. I went to the Berlin Book Fair as a best-selling author of three books, but without any invitation to discuss the translation of my books there. If it had not been for an invitation to go on to Italy which I took advantage of during the trip, it would have amounted to a transatlantic flight, one brief panel discussion then a transatlantic flight back the next day with no real thought given to what this meant for a black woman attending a literary event.

On the panel with me, there were four white men. I am not decrying the right of the other members of the panel to be there – one of them even has my deep affection – but I could not have felt more "at home". In Brazil it is a regular occurrence that a prominent panel will generate a certain embarrassment due to the lack of black people included there. This offers a beautiful excuse for the male white confraternity to continue to go

## WOMEN'S VOICES

on as before. Anyway, we were allotted only one hour for the panel, so each speaker would have only a short time to speak. First, the panel facilitator introduced the participants at the table one by one, and guess who he forgot to include? Embarrassed, he tried to improvise, showing that he knew little or nothing about me, in contrast to the respect shown for the men on the panel. So, I had to wait for the others to parade their arguments, each going over their allotted time, and then use the short time left to introduce myself as well as speak. Afterwards, there was a long queue of people lining up for me to autograph their copies of my books, even though nobody was interested in translating them into German.

Influential black rights activist Lélia Gonzalez has written that a black woman has to have both a first name and a surname, otherwise a racist will give her the name he wants to, so I spoke out about who I am. I said that I am a bestselling author in my home country, that I manage an independent publisher which in one year published eight black authors, and that I have been recognized as one of the 100 most influential women in the world, as well as being named a laureate in the Prince Claus Awards and so on. At the end, fellow Africans applauded, I think some white women found me arrogant, but I don't mind, because at a certain point in your life, coming from South America, you are no longer willing to eat crumbs for your dignity.

Being a black woman in Brazil you learn to deal with all the usual challenges that arise, but outside the borders of the country you face even higher barriers to progress due to a lack of knowledge and understanding of what happens north of Equador. In Brazil, black feminists are in a certain isolation due to language barriers - it is the only country in the Americas where Portuguese is the official language - to this is added the neo-colonial attitude that only what is produced in Europe or in the United States has any real worth, including, ironically, everything to do with decolonialization. In short, because of our position in the global geopolitical arrangement, the production of black Brazilian intellectuals tends to be much less widespread, causing delays in debates that could be much more advanced, especially if we think of countries that have a certain similarity to the historical construction of Brazilian racism.

## THE WOMEN WRITERS' HANDBOOK

After spending some time in France, Holland and Germany as well as in other countries, I could perceive a system at work to develop the foundations of racial democracy. If on the one hand, Brazil exported its particular brand of racist ideology, on the other hand some countries imported it. Who said that Brazil could only sell its state-owned companies?

Racism also occurs in micro-aggressions, in the "unsaid," as Kabengele Munanga, an important Congolese intellectual living in Brazil, defines it. The other day, I was in the airport of São Paulo, waiting to board my flight. A black woman there evokes surprise and some indignant looks. Sometimes people can't help themselves, as happened that day, when a woman sat next to me and started trying to hold a conversation. I wear headphones precisely to avoid this misfortune but that day it was no good. I took my headphones off and the first question she asked me was, "Are you going on board?" Well, I thought, I'm in the airport lounge, what else could I be doing there? Taking a break from cleaning, maybe? "Yes," I answered, monosyllabic. She wasn't satisfied and continued: "You're going to do what you've been doing abroad. Are you going dancing?" I said, "I'm not, why? Are you?" She was a bit taken aback and said, "Not me." "Well, neither am I."

Actually, I was on my way to Frankfurt to teach a class at Goethe University's Angela Davis college, but that wasn't likely to be the case for that poor woman. You see, there is no problem in going abroad to dance, there are various ways of expressing yourself and dance is certainly one of the most powerful and magnetic, especially in the Afro-Brazilian tradition, where dance is a way of speaking, celebrating and praying. I'm mentioning this because that woman thought that I could only be on my way to some country in the Northern Hemisphere if I were going there to dance. This is an illustrative example of the fixation of black women in places where the colonial gaze tolerates their existence. As a black Brazilian woman, I have to constantly deal with the stereotype of "export mulatto". It is even common when I am in Europe, alone, and come across a European man who at a certain moment in the conversation asks me where I am from, to which I answer Brazil, and I receive the animated reaction "Ah, Brazil!", as if I was going to samba for him at that exact moment.

## WOMEN'S VOICES

In that class at Goethe University, I introduced Lélia Gonzalez's reflections on the idea of Amefricanity, proposing an identity for the peoples of the Americas and the Caribbean. Even back in the 1980s, she was articulating the transnational struggle of the fellowship of black and indigenous women, questioning the imperialist parameters of black denominations in the American continent, in order to achieve a horizontal line of struggle.

> It's interesting to see someone who leaves Brazil, for example, saying they are going to "America". And that all of us, from any region of the continent, have repeated the same notion, perpetuating the imperialism of the United States, calling its inhabitants "Americans". And we, what are we, Asians?[4]

As for us blacks, how can we achieve an effective awareness of ourselves as descendants of Africans if we remain prisoners, "captives of a racist language"? That is why I propose that we use the term Amefricans to designate us all.

> Although we belong to different societies on the continent, we know that the system of domination is the same in all of them, that is: racism, this cold and extreme elaboration at all levels of thought, as well as part and parcel of the most different institutions of these societies. The political and cultural implications of the category of *Amefricanidade* (Amefricanity), are, in fact, democratic; precisely because the term itself allows us to overcome the limitations of territorial, linguistic and ideological character, opening new perspectives for a deeper understanding of that part of the world where it manifests itself: America as a whole (South, Central, North and Island)".[5]

Following in the footsteps of Lélia Gonzalez, I join with the Amefrican sisters to claim our identity in the American continent, so plundered over the years and whose violence continues to this day; a continent where within its borders, the violence arising from the capitalist, patriarchal,

---

4 & 5 Lélia Gonzalez. *The political-cultural category of Amefricanity. In Pensamento Feminista: conceitos fundamentais,* org. Heloisa Buarque de Almeida. Rio de Janeiro: Bazar do Tempo, (2019)

and racist system is increasingly sophisticated in order to remain in force with black and indigenous women at the base of society. However, even in the face of such an adverse scenario, the movement of African women is developing strategies of resistance, production, questioning, as well as that of love, dance, music for new civilizing milestones. In this transnational struggle of revolutionary affirmation for a dignified life, African and Afro-European women dance in a circle, among so many others moved by the feeling of transformation. I conclude with the words of Lélia Gonzalez, whose reading has encouraged me so much: "we not only share pain, but also the legacy of struggle."

Djamila Ribeiro

Brazilian human rights activist and author Djamila Ribeiro was born in the port city of Santos. She went on to study political philosophy at UNIFESP, one of the best universities in Brazil. Ribeiro is now one of the most popular writers and public figures in the Afro-Brazilian women's rights movement. Her blog has hundreds of thousands of followers and she regularly makes public appearances to discuss the lives of women in Brazil, a country in which people of colour experience exceptional levels of violence and prejudice. Her most recent book is *Nos, Madelenas: uma palavra pelo feminismo* (trans: *We Magdalenes:* a word for feminism).

In 2016, Ribeiro was appointed sub-secretary of Human Rights for the City of Sao Paulo, a position which she continues to hold. She was awarded a Master in Political Philosophy from the Federal University of São Paulo. Ribeiro is the author of *Lugar de Fala, Quem tem medo do Feminismo Negro?* and *Pequeno Manual Antirracista,* (still without translation into German). She is the Coordinator of the Plural Feminisms Collection, which fosters titles written by black people at an affordable price. A Laureate of the Prince Claus Award 2019 she was named one of the 100 most influential women in the world by the BBC.

*"Create whatever causes a revolution in your heart."*
— Elizabeth Gilbert

# INSPIRATION: WHERE DOES IT COME FROM?

## Fiona Rintoul

We've probably all had a Proustian moment, when a taste or smell catapults us back to the past. For me, those moments are often the starting point for a story.

The scent of a certain type of men's eau de cologne, for example, always teleports me to Paris, 1984. I catch the merest whiff of it, and I am once again 20 going on 21 and living the dream – eventually to become a nightmare – in the City of Light.

I pace Parisian boulevards and alleyways with a desire to get under the city's skin that borders on madness. Sitting on café terraces on the Place de l'Étoile sipping an espresso of an evening, I try desperately (and fail) to look French not Scottish. I make my coffee last two hours, to the irritation of the sniffy waiter, as I ogle the leggy prostitutes who open their fur coats and flash their naked bodies at the cars whizzing round the Arc de Triomphe. I am half-shocked, half-thrilled. East Kilbride this is not.

The eau de cologne belongs to my sort-of boyfriend. He is a car-crash blend of beauty, addiction and unresolved feelings for his godmother, whose photograph is tacked to the wall above his bed. I do not even begin to understand him, and he certainly doesn't understand me. But for the stories that doesn't matter. For he does not feature in the fiction his aftershave evokes.

## WOMEN'S VOICES

Instead, I write about Simone de Beauvoir. I understand now that she was the reason I went to Paris. I was trying to be her. My quest started well. As an English language assistant, I was assigned to the Lycée Camille Sée, where she used to teach. But it was of course doomed to failure.

Not for me a glamorous long-stay hotel in the Latin Quarter and afternoons spent penning memoirs in the Café des Deux Magots between contingent love affairs. Financial necessity propelled me into the employ of a Texan divorcee who lived in the sterile sixteenth arrondissement. In return for minimal au-pairing duties, which I hated, she provided me with an insanitary chambre de bonne next door to a fetid toilet on the top floor of her apartment building. There was a separate entrance for me and the Tunisian families who lived beside me in the attic. A steep, creaking fire hazard of a staircase led to our cramped quarters. Use of the main entrance and the lift was strictly forbidden.

The eau de cologne stories, then, are about broken dreams. About finding out that Paris is just a city like any other – though perhaps harder and less friendly than most.

That's the thing with those Proustian moments. They take you back, and then you start a new fictional journey, which might have little or nothing to do with what actually happened. The resulting fiction might, however, capture the essence of a time or place better than what actually happened.

That's certainly how it was for me when I wrote my novel *The Leipzig Affair*, which is set in the Communist East Germany of the 1980s. I studied German in Leipzig in 1986, but the novel is not the story of my time there. The idea for the novel began when I unearthed an old black-and-white photograph from a cupboard in my parents' house. It shows me crossing the main square in Leipzig's medieval centre with an East German friend. He's wearing a collarless open-neck shirt.

The sight of that shirt transported me back to Leipzig and to something he'd once told me: that he made all his own clothes because he didn't want to wear the shit you could buy in the East German shops. I used that detail as the starting point for Magda, the female protagonist in *The Leipzig Affair*.

From there, I built her character and her story. Just as the aftershave wearer doesn't feature in my Paris stories, the man in the photograph from

Leipzig doesn't feature in *The Leipzig Affair*. But my memory of him, which the photograph allowed me to access, was the catalyst for a new fictional journey to begin. And that new journey helped me to make sense of everything that I saw and heard and learnt in the Leipzig of before.

Much later, I realised that the book was also in some ways an homage to my old heroine, Simone de Beauvoir. It is modern history told through a series of love affairs, just like *The Mandarins*. In the novel I'm working on now, I've returned to that format, interlinking a series of affairs and passionate friendships to tell the story of a society in crisis.

Sometimes, of course, inspiration comes from present moments. You plunge forwards into an imagined future, rather than dipping back into the past. This happened to me recently in a café in Glasgow. I was sitting next to a young woman who was chatting to a friend on her phone. She was clearly on her way to an assignation, and I slowly realised that it had a transactional element – that she was part of one of the modern-day sugar daddy services you sometimes read about.

I pretended to read the paper, as she continued to chat. But I was clocking her every word. As soon as she left, I paid for my coffee and rushed home to get it all down on the computer.

Then I crafted it into fiction. By the time I'd finished, the story, which was published as *The Power of Pale* in *Gutter* magazine, had departed completely from the young woman in the café. Zoë, my protagonist, had a whole life that probably bears very little resemblance to the woman in the café's life. But without her, Zoë and her story would never have existed.

### Fiona Rintoul

Fiona Rintoul is the author of *The Leipzig Affair* (Aurora Metro), a novel set in the former East Germany, and *Whisky Island*, an exploration of the Isle of Islay and its whiskies. She is also translator of *Outside Verdun*, Arnold Zweig's anti-war classic set during the First World War.

*The Leipzig Affair* won the Virginia Prize for Fiction, was short-listed for the Saltire first book award and serialised on BBC R4's *Book at Bedtime*. As a journalist, Fiona contributes to a range of publications and is a regular book reviewer for the *Herald*. She lives in Glasgow and on the Isle of Harris.

# INTERVIEW WITH JASVINDER SANGHERA

Q. How did you come to write your first book?

A. As a young person who had experienced trauma one of my coping mechanisms was to write things down, so I would keep diaries and note books and pour out what lived silently within me. This was not with the objective of writing a book one day but a form of healing. However, as I began campaigning an agent spotted one of my articles in a national paper in which I was talking about women who had been murdered in dishonourable murders by family members. This person, Mark Lucas, wrote to me and suggested a meeting in which he felt that I had more to tell the world and the rest is history. I dug out every diary and went on the most cathartic journey that informed *Shame*. I gave more of me in this book than any other and chose to share some of the most vulnerable parts of my life because I felt it was important to be open and honest as there is no shame in vulnerability and making the wrong life choices. There were times when I had to put the writing down as it was painful, for example recalling and researching my sister Robina's suicide. This required me to visit the Coroner's office and that involved reading reports and seeing pictures of her burnt body as she set herself on fire. So, this book took longer to write but was so worthwhile not only for me but for the awareness it generated and even today I still hear of people who have been moved by the book.

## THE WOMEN WRITERS' HANDBOOK

I recently went to India and as I went through the passport control the female official looked at my picture and name and then me and she thanked me by putting her arms around me saying how she had read the book *Shame* and it gave her the courage to leave an abusive forced marriage and she has now saved herself and her daughters – WOW! It does not get better than that!

Q. What was the response?

A. After ten years of campaigning, forced marriage became a criminal offence in 2014. A part of me feels proud that the book definitely had something to do with that. When I met Samantha Cameron, she told me, "David still talks about that book." I was in a charity shop and saw the *Cameron on Cameron* book which has his personal interviews in it. One of the questions was: "What was the last book you read?" and the answer was my book *Shame*. The interview in the book explains why it made such an impression on him so I bought the *Cameron on Cameron* book and took it home.

Q. What were you hoping to do when you were growing up?

A. The place you wanted to be in when you grew up was never something that was discussed. What was encouraged was being prepared to become a wife and a daughter-in-law. You want to encourage your child, their aspirations and dreams – that was not happening. I witnessed some of my sisters being taken out of school at the age of 15 years old, forced to marry strangers. I was the next in line, as we got married in order of age. I had one sister younger than me. Whatever I wanted to be in my aspirations, they were futile.

When you grow up with this in your psyche, you don't have much freedom in your head to say, oh I'd like to be this, or I'd like to be that. The one thing I did want to be was an air hostess. The reason being, was it meant I could get out of that place and I could just travel the world. But that was more about wanting the freedom of getting out.

I left school with no qualifications whatsoever. I did not read a book until I was 27 years old. We were never encouraged to read and between the ages of 16 and 27, I was too busy surviving. When I was 27, I made the decision to educate myself, to do my A' Levels.

## WOMEN'S VOICES

Q. Which books have influenced you?

A. You know people always say, you don't choose the book, the book chooses you? The first book I ever read was Maya Angelou's *I Know Why a Caged Bird Sings*. It spoke to me on so many different levels and empowered me in so many different ways.

From college I went to university, got a first by the way, and I was pregnant in my final year! As I was doing all this, I was also campaigning. I established the charity Karma Nirvana in 1993 to give voice to the issues that I had experienced and create services for people who are misunderstood.

I got stronger and stronger, an education gave me the confidence to believe that I could do this, so Karma Nirvana became my life for 25 years. I made the very personal decision to step down as CEO in 2018. It took over everything. We began to develop services and a national day of remembrance is now in the British calendar to honour those who were murdered. The helpline that I started in my front room is now a national helpline; it has received over 89,000 calls since 2008. At the moment, it receives over 800 calls a month.

I was meeting with lots of survivors and that's how I developed the second book, *Daughters of Shame*. Very much by coming into contact with many survivors and seeking their permission to write their narratives, and there remain many stories to tell. There were many more than me and that was always the objective of *Daughters of Shame* – for people to understand that. That was where I developed a profession; I am now an expert witness in court. I gave evidence in the very first criminal trial of a mother being prosecuted for forcing her 13-year-old daughter into marriage – this is a British-born mother in Birmingham. I left Karma Nirvana in November 2018 as I decided it was time to go, and that was healthy.

The point is, I have done what I set out to achieve – it's a strong organisation. There are now civil and criminal laws to prevent forced marriage. It was time to go. In a way, I was putting all that pain into the books and organisation, so it almost became a form of therapy.

## THE WOMEN WRITERS' HANDBOOK

You've got to put that energy somewhere when you've been a survivor – do something – because you have been let down, you've been hurt, you've been abused. Or you can become angry, you can become unforgiving, all those things that you are absolutely entitled to feel, but for me I wasn't going to allow all that to become me, so I am who I am because of what happened to me and that's what I say to people.

**Q. What are you doing now?**

A. I want to continue writing. Writing requires discipline, time and research, energy. You can't just sit down 9 to 5 – it doesn't work like that. You have to work around the writing and how you feel; to put my energy into what I write, it has to have a purpose, an aim to help people understand something else. I'm interested in writing how these issues affect men and boys and how men and boys have a role. But also in children and young people in education and how we can increase awareness across our society.

Today I am writing but I am also the independent Safeguarding Chair for the children's board for Leeds city. I am also on the national Safeguarding Panel for the Church of England that seeks to reform the church and how it responds to and supports victims of sexual abuse. I believe there is a national gap in services for those people who have managed to put their head up from childhood and adult sexual abuse and there remains a need to acknowledge it and support rebuilding their lives. How ordinary people overcome the most extraordinary events: Trauma PTSD, developing the strategies to survive, is an area in which I am developing work, so watch this space!

**Q. What's the response from women and girls when you go into schools?**

A. They are willing to hear what you have to say and are very shocked by what they hear about it. I say very little now about my experience of overcoming the forced marriage. It's more of an inspirational talk about being somebody who's making a diffcrence for others and sharing my story of survival.

**Q. Do you think attitudes are changing in society towards forced marriage?**

## WOMEN'S VOICES

A. Absolutely. You are talking to a person who, in 1993 when I established the charity, I couldn't get more than one person to hear what I had to say. You know there were far more obstacles then. Now you have civil and criminal laws to protect people and so many more taking on this issue and developing effective responses.

In September this year, Relationship and Sex education will become compulsory in every school in England and Wales, and in that space, there is going to be the opportunity to talk about marriage. At the moment, I am also campaigning to raise the age of marriage from 16 to 18 to align with other countries. That campaign is gathering momentum because we have been having the conversation about child marriage and forced marriage. We have 43 police forces in the UK and 29 now have specialist forced marriage units within them, so things are changing.

**Q. How is social media and the internet helping?**

A. I always say in every presentation I do "please break our silences" and you break it by talking about it and that means social media, be it Facebook or Twitter or websites. That has been the gateway to holding the conversation, but also to provincial victims or survivors engaging with organisations and helplines as well, and that's really, really important.

I know that in term of referrals to help lines and services they don't just come through professionals they come through self-referrals and that is because somebody has spread a tweet or their friend has put something up and also those people in positions of power and influence – so celebrities, lets say – they could tweet something and it could completely change how somebody looks at this or engages with a service and so absolutely that has been a gateway to raising awareness. Let's not forget, you know, criminalising forced marriage national day of remembrance – it was a twitter campaign that started it.

**Q. What's next? Any more books?**

A. I do want to explore the whole thing around men and the role of men. I've just come back from India and looked at some fascinating work and the conversation they are having at the moment because of the rapes there of women and men. People in the villages are standing up and taking a stand. That's what I am interested in at the moment. I am interested in writing about the experiences of men but also the role of men and boys in tackling the issue so look out for that one.

## Jasvinder Sanghera CBE

Jasvinder Sanghera was born and brought up in Derby. A survivor of a forced marriage, she is the founder of Karma Nirvana, an award-winning charity that supports both men and women affected by honour-based abuse and forced marriages. Her memoir *Shame* was described in the House of Lords as a 'political weapon' and, along with *Daughters of Shame*, are *Sunday Times'* Top 10 Bestsellers.

In 2018, she was awarded an Honorary Doctor of Law by De Montfort University, Leicester, and Woman of the Year by Leeds City Council. In 2019, she was awarded the Robert Burns Humanitarian of the Year Award and also the Sikh Woman of Substance Award. Sanghera is recognised as bringing the issue of forced marriage into the public domain and Prime Minister David Cameron stated that her work 'turned my head on the issue of forced marriage'.

> "There's really no such thing as the 'voiceless'. There are only the deliberately silenced, or the preferably unheard."
> – Arundhati Roy

# A ROOM OF ONE'S OWN...
# OR NOT?

## Anne Sebba

Sitting, standing, working or simply being alone is a necessary condition for any writer. At least relatively alone. Some journalists are able to block out the background noises of a hectic newsroom and be alone in their heads to find the stillness and stimulation necessary to create. Luckily, I trained in such a noisy, frenetic newsroom in the days when Fleet Street was synonymous with such places. I worked alongside reporters, often called firemen, never firewomen, who really did wear trench coats and dangled cigarettes as if they had just emerged from the set of a Hollywood detective movie. There were no remotely female-friendly shops or cafés, just smoky pubs, where "a lead" or "a scoop" were discussed. It was the early 1970s, less than 30 years after the end of World War II. Yet I failed to realize how close it was to that war, until I had to do nightshifts and would park just below St Paul's in a bomb crater repurposed as a large open car park. On those occasions, the graveyard shift, the news floor was truly silent. But the rest of the time the shouting and bustle, fury and adrenaline (or was it testosterone?) trained me not to be precious about needing silence. But silence is precisely that: precious.

My first full-length book after I left Reuters (or, more correctly, after they asked me to leave when they learned I was pregnant) was a biography of the novelist and playwright Enid Bagnold[6], a Sussex neighbour of

6 Titled *Enid Bagnold: A Life*.

## WOMEN'S VOICES

Virginia Woolf who longed for Woolf's admiration. I learnt from Bagnold as much about the art of writing itself as about carving out the time to write. If I could only have imbibed by osmosis the way she eschewed clichés. Her own birth she described as "sperm shot across two centuries to arrive at me". Such an earthy — and original — simile was typical of her prose, which she once described as "beautiful vomit". But she also gave practical advice to mothers trying to write with children at home in the days before going to a coffee shop to set up your laptop was the norm. Go into your study, she advised, assuming every woman had such a room, and close the door, whether you are writing or not. Find something to work at even if just a letter. Today social media makes this all too easy, but of course is usually little more than a distraction, displacement activity.

And yet recently (with age?) I have started to think differently about needing absolute silence. Now that I have so much of it, I am not sure I am so keen on it. After all, I am often the one to speak out loud while writing, recognizing that sometimes I need to hear how the cadence works. Let's agree for the moment, ninety years after Virginia Woolf herself wrote her ground-breaking text, about the inviolable principle of a room of one's own, especially for a woman who may be able to write only in the snatched interstices of a day caring for children. But when we emerge from that room just how much interaction is useful with readers?

What about another room in which to share what you have written? Although nobody else but you is going to create the book, article or short story, many writers find some measure of collaborative effort and discussion (or just plain editing) a necessary spur or corrective. Most writers strike a balance; do the initial creating alone but have a first reader — a spouse, partner, professional editor or grown child with whom to discuss what you've written. (Although perhaps it's not such a good idea to be in the same room when this first reader reads. Shouldn't you let them undertake this poisoned chalice of a task alone, out of earshot of any grimaces or groans?)

How do I manage this balance of solitariness versus the rest of life? I invent small treats or rewards for myself, as insignificant as going to the local supermarket. Sometimes I go for walks in Richmond either along the river or through the park and since I live within a stone's throw of

## THE WOMEN WRITERS' HANDBOOK

where Virginia herself lived and worked – Hogarth House in the, for her, not so aptly named Paradise Road – it is hard not to wonder if the source of my peace of mind and inspiration was ever a source for her? Since she produced some of her finest work during the decade she was here I cannot believe that Richmond was wholly inimical to her creativity. Or I give lectures around the country and travel to research information which may well be extraneous to my overall subject, simply to make sure I have some interaction with the rest of the world. I like it when other people say to me: "Have you read this book? Have you thought of that approach? Have you considered interviewing X?" Sometimes I might even take my laptop to work on in bed ... it's a temporary room of my own, but I like to feel the vibrations of life elsewhere in the household.

But there is, of course, a difference to being alone and total isolation, and most of my writer friends dislike total isolation but crave being alone in short bursts.

All of this has been brought into sharp focus for me by my current preoccupation: I am writing a biography of a woman sent to prison in 1951, living in solitary confinement for the last two years of her life, who wrote to her husband in another part of the prison, regular letters of powerful emotional depth and (in my view) some literary ability. Both Julius and Ethel Rosenberg had been condemned to death for conspiracy to commit espionage and could see each other only once a week, when he was brought to sit in a cage next to her cell. Yet, when the letters were published, some liberal, anti-communist critics criticised Ethel's style as "petit bourgeois" or "full of bathos" or complained that she tried too hard because she used a dictionary to find a more unusual word and a notebook to store phrases. It's a salutary reminder for me that what I may consider being alone is a far cry from this – total isolation. I find it extraordinary that she wrote at all, that she (mostly) kept her spirits above the lowest depression level and functioned as a dignified human being with fire in her belly and integrity. Pretentious? Striving for effect? What writer doesn't strive for that, whether in a room of one's own, or a cell, or a crowded noisy café? We may need a room of our own most of the time, but we need to feel the vibrations of life as well. Some of us need that more than others.

# WOMEN'S VOICES

**Anne Sebba**

Anne Sebba is an award-winning biographer, historian and author of eleven books. Her latest, *Les Parisiennes: How the Women of Paris Lived, Loved and Died in the 1940s* was awarded the 2016 Franco-British Society book prize. Previously, she wrote *That Woman*, a biography of Wallis Simpson. A former Reuters Foreign Correspondent, Sebba is also a broadcaster who regularly appears on television talking about her books, mostly biographies including Jennie Churchill, Mother Teresa, William Bankes and Laura Ashley. She is a former chair of Britain's 10,000 strong Society of Authors, an accredited 'Arts Society' lecturer and Senior Research Fellow at the Institute of Historical Research. She is currently working on a biography of Ethel Rosenberg (publication UK and US 2021).

# BEING A FEMINIST WRITER

## Kalista Sy

My name is Khadidiatou Sy, but I'm better known as Kalista Sy, it's my armour-plating. I am what you might call an outsider, a pure product of Senegalese society. I come from the bottom rung of the ladder; we're part of a wave of Senegalese people who've held out because they had dreams.

One day I had the deep conviction that I'd be able to make a success of my life and that whatever I needed, I would be able to buy it for myself. Without realizing it, I had become a "Feminist".

Whenever I advocate for the financial empowerment of women, I am considered to be a feminist. This doesn't bother me because now, in 2020, the definition of feminism is that we should all have the same chances in life, whether we are male or female.

I am the great, great-granddaughter of a strong woman: La Grande-Royale. A woman who knew how to achieve what she wanted and keep to her beliefs. Like her, I carry the pride, the values and the conviction to do what needs to be done. Because for me, if we want to make women strong, we must show them images of strong women. And in this way, deconstruct the male view of our bodies. It is my belief that only those who struggle can make their dreams come true.

When I wanted to tell a woman's story and depict my daily life in my writing, I knew that it would be a bit disturbing. In the TV series I wrote titled *Mistress of a married Man*, I showed the kind of women we all know, the women we care about. Watching the majority of drama series on

## WOMEN'S VOICES

television that are written by men, I felt strongly that it was time that what is shown on television reflects our reality.

I wanted to hear and see those women who have never been given a voice before. It seemed to me that what was generally portrayed on TV has nothing to do with ordinary women and that there was a desire to carefully avoid any subjects that reflect our daily lives, or depict what we are really like.

By following the lives of five women characters in my TV series, audiences around the world are discovering that we have something in common with people who, at first glance, seem very far away from us. The magic is that the viewer naturally identifies with a character. Telling the stories of these women brings minority characters to the forefront to broaden the scope of the representation of women. The diversity of characters in the series makes it possible for everyone to identify with them.

What has been difficult for me, is realizing that there are still many people today who judge the choices that some women make about their sexuality, their future...

Maybe one of the traits I picked up from my great, great grandmother La Grande-Royale, is that I'm not the kind of woman who adheres to the model of women that men would like us to emulate.

There's this question that keeps coming up over and over again: Why did you write it?

I chose to write it because I knew it had to be done. I did it to show my daughter that she can decide, that she can say things, that she has the right to be herself.

I did it because at one point I was afraid I wouldn't have the right to say what's in my heart and how I see the women around me.

It is important to me that women always feel in control. They shouldn't feel that they can't or shouldn't be something in life. I don't want them to think that they can't or shouldn't try. Because we are capable, we are so capable.

## THE WOMEN WRITERS' HANDBOOK

I felt the need to start a movement that could change things. It may be that one day I will again feel fear. After a very painful experience, I lost my brother, my little sister, my best friend. I knew then that I would never be silenced again and that I would tackle the difficult subjects in my work.

My job is to bring out what is within. It takes courage and vulnerability.

There are times when I say to myself: am I not exposing my family? But my family, my friends, my loved ones all know that without this inner conviction driving me, I don't exist.

They'd rather see me live by taking risks than die without lifting a finger. By doing this work I learn things that are important every day. Especially achieving small victories over those things that are important to us.

Sometimes it doesn't seem like you are winning. Sometimes winning is just about showing courage...

What we fight for every day is to have a choice. When I write, I have the choice and the power to change things and I enjoy using it. And I also give my women characters the ability to make a lot of choices for their lives.

And to all those women who doubt their ability, I show them myself as a smiling example, one drop of water in the bucket of potentialities. And I tell them that talent has no gender, it has no sex.

It all depends on our determination as women: a woman president exists, as does a woman engineer, a scientist, a lawyer, a judge, a footballer, a boxer, a scriptwriter, a decision-maker; there are women achieving things everywhere.

Today I dare to be myself and I dare to dream that all women will have the same opportunity one day. What I want to do now is to work with young women and girls, to show them that this is possible.

There is a lot of talk about economic development and women's empowerment. I believe that this will only be possible if Female Leadership is very strong. When more women are represented, it will allow greater access to education, training and skills.

Today, I remain true to myself through my work. I speak out to challenge the male gaze on the female body and I don't censor myself for others.

## WOMEN'S VOICES

I know it won't be easy and it won't be without risks, but I like doing this. And I know that I have opened a door and that many will follow me through it with opportunities and hope.

In my work, I promote women. I put them in positions that used to be reserved for men and I ask them to believe in themselves and to give their all. And they do and they succeed.

I come from the bottom rung of the ladder. I have lived through misery, poverty and I felt angry. I refused to marry a rich man just to have a good opening in society.

Instead, I believed in myself and today when I buy things, I do it with my own money. The money I make from working. Now I tell women: "Be true to yourself and believe in your abilities."

**Kalista Sy**

Kalista Sy is a Senegalese screenwriter, notable for writing and producing the TV series *Mistress of a married Man (Maîtresse d'un Homme marié)* from 2016–2020, set in Dakar. The series is broadcast on Marodi TV Sénégal and is also available on YouTube.

"...the series puts women's experiences at the center of its storyline. Marème and her cohort are ambitious women with jobs and their lives do not center exclusively on their relationships with men." – Professor Marame Gueye

The series' frank discussion of female sexual freedom led to Islamic clerics calling for it to be banned.

In 2019, Sy was listed among the BBC's 100 Most Influential Women.

"Be Kind. Be Connected. Be Unafraid."

– Rivera Sun

# MSLEXIA: ARE WE CURED YET?

## Debbie Taylor

Just over twenty years ago, in the inaugural issue of *Mslexia* magazine, I highlighted the glaring disparity between women's potential as writers and our actual achievements – and invented a new word, 'mslexia', to describe the phenomenon. In a nutshell, women study literature in far greater numbers than men, read far more books, and attend more writing courses. All things being equal, we should dominate every prize shortlist and bestseller chart, and run every publishing company. The data we gathered at that time demonstrated that was very far from the case.

Back in 1999, men were twice as likely as women to be published, twice as likely to be reviewed, twice as likely to win major fiction awards, nine times as likely to win poetry prizes. Crucially, men were also 25 per cent more likely to submit their manuscripts to agents, editors and grant awarding bodies.

A quick glance at the literary landscape today suggests things have changed dramatically for the better since then. Women won this year's Booker, Forward and Carnegie awards and crowded onto the shortlists of most other major literary prizes. Does this mean we've achieved parity at last? Is mslexia a thing of the past?

Sadly not. Though the success of increasing numbers of brilliant women writers has laid the foundations of a more feminised literary canon and provided a slew of new role models for younger women, those achievements don't mean mslexia has gone away, any more than the

## THE WOMEN WRITERS' HANDBOOK

Obama presidency spelled an end to bigotry in the US. A few dazzling swallows do not a summer make.

No one would dare argue that the success of black authors such as Jackie Kay, Malorie Blackman and Kamila Shamsie means there isn't an issue for Black, Asian and Minority Ethnic (BAME) writers. It takes more than a lusty crop of Mantels to prove that everything's hunky-dory in the garden of women's writing.

The problem is, whenever an advance is made, there's a tendency for society to mop its brow and wash its hands of the issue. So does mslexia, as we defined it in 1999, still exist?

First, are men still more likely to be published? With the number of new titles each year in the US alone nudging a third of a million, it's impossible to know exactly. But Ruth Franklin's team at *The New Republic* had a stab at it, looking at 13 US publishers who produced fiction and non-fiction of the type eligible to be reviewed – and found that 68 per cent of titles were by men.

If men are still more likely to be published in high-status genres, it's not surprising that they are also more likely to be reviewed. Our 'Review of the reviews' in 2000 found that men's books were twice as likely as women's to be reviewed in the UK and that men were three times as likely to be reviewers. Since 2009, the annual 'VIDA count' has taken up the baton and found little has changed in the intervening years.

Though the VIDA figures shamed some publications into reviewing their editorial policies, a recent analysis of the language used in reviews of women's books is a cause for concern. US academics Andrew Piper and Richard Jean So analysed 10,287 reviews published in the flagship *New York Times* Book Review since 2000 and commented that it was like being 'jettisoned back into a linguistic world that more nearly resembles our Victorian ancestors'. Book reviewers were over three times more likely to use 'domestic' words such as 'marriage', 'mother', 'love' and 'beauty' about women's books, and twice as likely to use 'ideas' words such as 'leader', 'argument' and 'theory' about men's books – regardless of the subject matter of the books concerned.

## WOMEN'S VOICES

As Piper and So conclude: 'Women writers are still being defined by their "sentimental" traits... while men are defined by their attention to matters of science and the state'. No prizes for guessing which traits are considered more important.

Talking of prizes, let's take a closer look at those literary prizes, where women are at last beginning to make serious inroads. Back in 2002 we analysed the style and subject matter of ten Booker Prize-winning novels from 1990-2000 – and discovered that nearly all were written in the third person and had a male protagonist. Yes, including the books written by women. In 2015, author Nicola Griffith brought that research up to date and found exactly the same thing: 12 of the 15 Booker winners from 2000-2014 had a male protagonist. And this was true of all the major literary awards she looked at, causing her to conclude: 'the more prestigious, influential and financially remunerative the award, the less likely the winner is to write about grown women.'

In my *Mslexia* article on 'The masculine aesthetic' in 2002, I argued that because men had been the gatekeepers of literature for centuries – running every book publisher, magazine and newspaper – what has historically been deemed excellent has been synonymous with what men like. And what they like, as survey after survey shows to this day, is writing by and about men.

Easy-peasy, I can hear you saying. All we need to do is change the gatekeepers. Well, actually the gatekeepers have changed somewhat in recent years. Though our own research this year found that women were in charge of only a third of literary magazines, women have long been in the majority employed in mainstream publishing, and it's rare to find an all-male literary judging panel.

Yet there is little evidence that women judges automatically favour women. Most investigations show that most male readers are virtually phobic about books by women. A recent survey by Goodreads of 40,000 people found 90 per cent of men's top 50 books were by male authors. Women judges and readers are pretty even-handed by comparison. What this means, of course, is that any judging panel with equal numbers of men and women on it, will still end up choosing a majority of books by and about men.

## THE WOMEN WRITERS' HANDBOOK

This is why the more closely a woman writer can approximate to the masculine aesthetic, the more likely she is to succeed. No wonder – as our own surveys have repeatedly demonstrated – we have so little confidence in our writing; no wonder we hesitate to submit our work; no wonder we are so discouraged when we are rejected. The cards really are stacked against us.

If you doubt my words, consider the experience of novelist Catherine Nichols, who sent out her novel to 50 (male and female) agents and received just two requests to read the whole manuscript. But when, as 'George', she submitted the same covering letter and pages to 50 agents, 17 agents wanted to see the whole book. 'George is eight and a half times better than me at writing the same book,' she says. What's more, the feedback she was getting as 'Catherine' praised her 'beautiful writing', while 'George' was praised for being 'clever' and 'exciting'. As Catherine, she says, 'I was being conditioned like a lab animal against ambition'. Which led her to wonder to what extent other writers were having their individuality stifled and being steered onto the restrictive tramlines of 'women's fiction'.

That's certainly what Meg Wolitzer believes. In the *New York Times* Book Review, she argues that diverse books by women tend to be segregated and lumped together as 'women's fiction', and so prevented from 'entering the larger, more influential playing field'. Publishers perpetuate this bias by packaging women's books so that they appear less weighty – with 'domestic' imagery on the covers, for instance – and reviewers follow suit, in both the quantity and subtext of their coverage. As *The New Republic* editor Ruth Franklin remarks in 'Why the literary landscape continues to disadvantage women', 'we have gained admission to the world of men... but admission is not the same thing as acceptance'.

Here is how prize-winning author Claire Vaye Watkins summed up the situation in her essay 'On pandering' in Tin House last year:

'Nearly all of my life has been arranged around... watching boys, emulating them, trying to catch the attention of the ones who have no idea I exist.

## WOMEN'S VOICES

'I watched Melville, I watched Salinger, watched Ford, Flaubert, Díaz, Dickens... I read women, but I didn't watch them... I have built a working miniature replica of the patriarchy in my mind. Countless decisions I've made about what to write and how to write it have been in acquiescence to the opinions of the white male literati.

'About a year ago I had a baby, and while my life was suddenly more intense, more frightening, more beautiful, more difficult, and more profound than it had ever been, I found myself with nothing to write about... I thought I had enough material for a novel but when it came out it was a short story, and one that felt unserious... Nothing's happening to me [I thought]. I need to go shoot an elephant.

'But I don't want to write like a man any more. I don't want to be praised for being "unflinching." I want to flinch. I want to be wide open.'

So say all of us.

**Debbie Taylor**
Debbie Taylor is the founder and Editorial Director of *Mslexia*. She has worked as Editor at *New Internationalist* and *Writing Women* magazines and as a writer, researcher and project manager for many organisations, including Oxfam, Anti-Slavery, BBC 2, Channel 4, UNICEF and WHO. Her novels include *The Fourth Queen* and *Hungry Ghosts*. She lives in a decommissioned lighthouse at the mouth of the Tyne with her husband and daughter.

# MY MOTHER, READING A NOVEL

## Madeleine Thien

1

I have no memory of my mother ever reading a novel. She read newspapers, recipes and textbooks, bills and manuals.

But my mother sitting on the sofa, holding a book in her hand, lost in a novel – I cannot recall ever seeing this.

And yet –

I find it easy to close my eyes and imagine such a scene. Here is my mother: she wears a green cardigan with a needle and a bit of thread pinned into it, her glasses slip down her nose, she has a finger on the tip of a page. She is reading. She has forgotten that I am here. She's gone away to somewhere none of us can follow. And when she looks up from the book, for a second she doesn't know where she is. Or, momentarily, who she is. Something is alive in her that was not alive just a few pages before.

My mother was thirty years old when she arrived in Canada with a five-year-old son and a three-year-old daughter. It was 1974. It was winter. Did she feel, as Virginia Woolf once described a character, as if "a thousand softly padded doors" had closed behind her? I think that she did. I see my mother, who was pregnant with me, step out of the airport and into another life. My mother had twenty-eight more years to live. She would return to Asia once, briefly, to visit her family in Hong Kong, and when she came back, she would tell me, "Never go home to a place that needs you less than you need it."

## WOMEN'S VOICES

In Canada, my mother did not have time to read novels. Reading novels would not buy bread or pay the rent. One had to accept the sheer necessity of feeding, clothing and organizing children, of getting to one's job and then one's second job and third job. More times than I can count, I found my mother asleep at the dining table. Having come home late, she had fallen asleep on her curved arm, immediately after finishing her evening meal, or having a cup of tea, or sitting down to rest.

When she died, I asked one of my aunts, "What was my mother like as a girl?" My aunt surprised me. She said, "Your mother loved to read. In between school and work, she was always reading stories." I asked what books she loved, and my aunt said, "She loved a famous novel called *Dream of the Red Chamber.*" My mother had kept this book on our shelves all these years, but because I could not read Chinese, I had not recognized it as a novel. I had not known what kind of book it was.

2

"But I have sometimes thought," wrote Edith Wharton, "that a woman's nature is like a great house full of rooms: there is the hall, through which everyone passes in going in and out; the drawing-room, where one receives formal visits; the sitting-room, where the members of the family come and go as they list; but beyond that, far beyond, are other rooms, the handles of whose doors perhaps are never turned; no one knows the way to them, no one knows whither they lead; and in the inner-most room, the holy of holies, the soul sits alone and waits for a footstep that never comes."[7]

This passage has lived in my mind for decades. On the one hand is the loneliness – the footstep that never comes – and on the other, the sacredness, the holy of holies, of the innermost room whose door remains unopened. What if we aren't waiting for someone else to open it? What if it is we, ourselves, who never find the room, or go in search of it, who never approach and turn the handle?

In the novels we read when we are young, we use our minds to push open a door. We enter a realm that is ever changing. We leap through

---

[7] *The Fullness of Life* by Edith Warton (1893)

## THE WOMEN WRITERS' HANDBOOK

time and across space, and descend into the vastness of another mind. We speak words that were born inside another person, and we fall outside of the consciousness of ourselves, only to wake up, on the other side of the door, exhilarated or weeping or trembling.

Reading this deeply is a spooky experience, isn't it? As if someone called out a different name and you answered it, because the story was real and you were fictional.

In my twenties, I walked through the stories of Alice Munro as if they, too, were my home, as if I had grown up knowing all too well the fields, skies, shops, parlours and factories of Huron County. There are stories of hers that I have read dozens of times, climbing staircases I thought I knew – only to be plummeted into a room I hadn't expected, and jolted into the light. "Words most wished for can change," wrote Alice Munro. "Something can happen to them, while you are waiting. Love – need – forgive. Love – need – forever. The sound of such words," she writes, "can become a din, a battering in the street. And all you can do is run away, so as not to honour them out of habit."[8]

I can find no word to adequately describe the ones who came before. Ancestors, forebears, predecessors, precursors, parents, what to call them? All these writers who picked me up, disoriented me and set me down. I'm almost afraid to admit this –

Alice Munro taught me some of my deepest lessons about feminism. Her girls and women are flawed, jealous, full of pride and illusions, lustful, tender, violent. They are liars, schemers and truth-tellers, victims, survivors, geniuses, mothers, widows, daughters, loners – they are human, with all the humour, joy, fickleness, cruelty, superficiality and tragedy of the human condition. It is because they are all these things, not in spite of it, that wisdom comes in bursts and flares.

Her books, and by extension, the library, are like half-lit, shadowed rooms in which we keep bumping into one another, and into ourselves. My literary forebears are men, women, people – people who have undone some curtain and revealed another puzzle of the world. They write about sexuality, violence, language and history, love and freedom. The gender

8 *The Jack Randa Hotel* by Alice Munro in *The New Yorker*, July 19, 1993 P. 62

## WOMEN'S VOICES

of the writer was important to me, yes, but more important was the acuteness with which they could perceive, observe and describe some part of existence. Virginia Woolf put it this way: "I was always going to the bookcase for another sip of the divine specific."

Modern novelists, Virginia Woolf observed in 1925, do not write better than their predecessors. "We do not come," she wrote, "to write better; all that we can be said to do is to keep moving, now a little in this direction, now in that, but with a circular tendency..."

Edith Wharton's great house full of rooms is also a place of hallways, doorways and passages. Foyers and side rooms where generations overlap, in which we break like waves against each other – waves of feminism perhaps – sometimes brutally, sometimes forcefully or indifferently, but always with a kind of implacable pattern, part of the same substance no matter the frictions – individual, political, national – pulling us apart.

3

Predecessors, forebears, parents. For the last ten years I have been writing about the aftermath of war and war's beginnings. I've written about the civil war and the genocide in Cambodia, which took place when I was a child. After finishing that novel, I had so many difficult questions – questions about ideology and revolution, about social justice and solidarity, and the price we should pay, or should not pay to bring about radical change. And this led me to think deeply about China's Cultural Revolution and the 1989 Tiananmen demonstrations.

During the Cultural Revolution, a generation of students was told to destroy the old world in order to bring about the new. What came under attack was the world of history, memory, knowledge and family. A piece of music, a work of literature, a poem that once moved you, or a letter from your father who might be a class enemy – these were forbidden, for they seeped into your being and rewired the way you experienced the time in which you were alive. They made you doubt. According to Chairman Mao, art for art's sake, love for love's sake, was a crime; all art and love must serve the prevailing orthodoxy.

## THE WOMEN WRITERS' HANDBOOK

Thirty-six million people would be targeted, and hundreds of thousands would lose their lives. The many suicides by musicians, teachers, professors, scholars, scientists and workers – by parents and grandparents – reflected profound despair and perhaps an inability, or a refusal, to accept the Cultural Revolution's world of absolutes.

Only the young, Mao argued, had the courage to destroy old customs, habits, culture and ideas. Burn it all down, he told them, destroy it, and throw it in the trash.

The horrific tragedy of the Cultural Revolution is difficult to encapsulate in words. It was a lie – told to a generation of young people who were willing to put their bodies on the line for their ideals. Mao insisted that every generation must build the world anew and that power comes from the barrel of a gun. He said that those who want a better world have not only the right but the obligation to enact violence on others. The revolution turned people against people, individuals against individuals, but left the overall power structure intact. As the country descended into chaos, Mao remained safe in power.

4

Virginia Woolf frequently uses images of doorways in her novels. Doors to move between interior and exterior, present and past, literal and metaphorical, one generation and the next – the doorway says that there is no fixed wall between what came before and what is arriving now, "no unbreachable gap", as the critic Marion Dell writes. These words seem like a prayer to me and a manifesto: there is no unbreachable gap.

We are living in a precarious moment, I have come to believe.

Virginia Woolf saw this acutely, she saw it in her own time. "It is hate, it is love," she wrote in *The Waves*. "That is the furious coal-black stream that makes us dizzy if we look down into it. We stand on a ledge here, but if we look down we turn giddy.... It is love ... it is hate," she writes. "But our hatred is almost indistinguishable from our love."

"Love of the world," wrote Hannah Arendt. "Why is it so difficult to love the world?" And yet, she realized, the things we hate are things we seek to dispose of. So what political action is possible unless we do,

## WOMEN'S VOICES

in fact, love this world? She argued for passionate thinking, which she defined as "judgment without scorn, truth-finding without zeal."

In the opening of his novel, *In the Skin of a Lion*, Michael Ondaatje quotes the *Epic of Gilgamesh*, as Gilgamesh mourns the death of Enkidu, his brother, soulmate and friend:

"The joyful will stoop with sorrow," Gilgamesh weeps, "and when you have gone to the earth, I will let my hair grow long for your sake, I will wander through the wilderness in the skin of a lion." In his mourning, Gilgamesh clothes himself even more deeply in the things of this world.

Hannah Arendt, Virginia Woolf, Alice Munro, Edith Wharton, Michael Ondaatje – I keep returning to the words of others, to my literary forebears. Perhaps because I'm a novelist, and a novel is a place of ideas, a juxtaposition of different voices, a labyrinth of voices. "The complexity of things – the things within things – " as Alice Munro says, "just seems to be endless."

If Edith Wharton's observation is acute and true, "that a woman's nature is like a great house full of rooms ... and in the innermost room, the holy of holies, the soul sits alone and waits for a footstep that never comes,"[9] then perhaps the work of our predecessors and forebears, those who come before, has been to move us ever closer to that hidden room, that holy of holies. We cannot find it on our own. Millennia of life and thinking have come before us, each one feeling its way through the labyrinth, men and women together, people stumbling against one another, sometimes hurting one another, sometimes carrying one another, closer to the surface.

\*

One day, when I was 26, I received a phone message telling me that something had happened to my mother and I should wait for further news. I was cold and afraid. I climbed into bed at a loss. I picked up the book I had been reading and opened it up. The book was a novel, *Cees Nooteboom's All Souls Day*, and this is the exact passage I read at that moment:

9 *The Fullness of Life* by Edith Wharton (1893)

## THE WOMEN WRITERS' HANDBOOK

"The graveyard was so big that you couldn't see where it ended... Perhaps the graveyard itself was floating, sailing like a ship of joy through the air. Any moment now it would rise up and take the women, the children, and the flowers on a journey through space."

The phone rang and I went to answer it. It was my sister telling me that my mother had died in her sleep. My mother was 58 years old. She had been caught in a job that saddened her, harassed by a supervisor she despised, she had been the target of racist and abusive behaviour. She had kept meticulous notes, and spoken often of retirement, of wanting to rest.

What did I feel then? Aside from the profound pain of losing her, I felt that I had failed her. A daughter should be able to protect her mother. I know that she felt proud of me. My daughter is a writer, she would say. My daughter has words and there are people who know her name. My daughter belongs, truly belongs, to another world from me.

In the sixteen years since my mother died, I have kept that *Cees Nooteboom* novel close to me. In fact, I have never read the last few pages even though it is one of my most beloved books. For me the novel will never end, will always be interrupted, will always carry a text that I know is beyond my reach. I imagine that my mother ripped the last few pages out and took them with her. And now it was up to me to go on, to live out the rest of my adult life.

When my father died a few months ago, my heart was broken. His life was complex, full of heartache, severe depression and also joy. I cannot properly describe the pride and joy he took in my life. He believed I had mastered the language which had so often failed him. I remembered how he carried my library books from the car into the house, how he laid them down on my bed with such tenderness and curiosity, books he never read, until, near the end of his life, he finished my nearly 500-page novel, *Do Not Say We Have Nothing*. And when his partner, my stepmother, asked him why certain characters in the novel could not save one another, or the music they loved, my father answered, "They did the best they could in the time they had, under the circumstances in which they lived."

My literary forebears, ancestors, predecessors, precursors, do not know how intertwined they are in the lives of my parents. Nor, I think, did my

## WOMEN'S VOICES

parents ever know how much they were seen and imagined by the writers I loved as I was growing up.

In a story, Alice Munro writes of the children in fairy stories, "...who have seen their parents make pacts with terrifying strangers, who have discovered that our fears are based on nothing but the truth, who come back ... dazed and powerful with secrets."[10]

I ran away from my parents, much like a young woman in an Alice Munro story. And when I was ready, and they were ready, I came back home.

I do not think that literature's primary role is to educate or to teach. But I do think that I learned many forms of forgiveness, which is a kind of love, through the novels and stories that cut me most deeply. Our fears are based on nothing but the truth, Munro writes. And that truth might be that we – parents and children – are frail and deeply flawed. That we are full of love that sometimes takes a selfless and beautiful shape, and sometimes takes a selfish and violent shape. We must somehow learn to perceive the difference. As long as we live, said Hannah Arendt, this is the ground given to us "though it seems to be a battlefield and not a home." But to imagine this place only as a battlefield and not a home will not suffice. "Understanding," Arendt writes, "is unending and therefore cannot produce final results. It is the specifically human way of being alive; for every single person needs to be reconciled to a world into which she was born a stranger."

It feels fitting to end with Alice Munro, and so this is an extract from the ending of my favourite story *The Jack Randa Hotel*:

"Hundreds, maybe thousands, of butterflies were hanging in the trees, resting before their long flight down the shore of Lake Huron and across Lake Erie, then on south to Mexico. They hung there like metal leaves, beaten gold – like flakes of gold tossed up and caught in the branches.

Love – forgive

Love – forget

Love – forever

Hammers in the street."[11]

10  *The Shining Houses* (in *Dance of the Happy Shades*) by Alice Munro
11  *The Jack Randa Hotel* by Alice Munro in *The New Yorker*, July 19, 1993 p. 62

## THE WOMEN WRITERS' HANDBOOK

*This essay was originally delivered as the keynote address of the 2018 Alice Munro Festival of the Short Story in Huron County, Ontario.*

**Madeleine Thien**

Madeleine Thien is perhaps best known for her epic novel *Do Not Say We Have Nothing* (2016), which spans the length of China's modern history from Mao's revolution in 1949 to the Cultural Revolution in the late 1960s to Tiananmen Square in 1989. The novel won the 2016 Governor General's Award and the Scotiabank Giller Prize in Canada.

# INTERVIEW WITH CLAIRE TOMALIN

Q. **What drew you to the subjects of your biographies?**
A. Well, women's lives haven't always been described as well as they could be. For one thing, when I was at Cambridge, I was studying Dickens, and this was back in 1952, and I saw biographies of Dickens which seldom mentioned that there was this little actress he knew, and they just said she failed his need and she was mean and mercenary. I thought then that they're not interested in her. If she was twelve years with Dickens, why don't they ask where she came from or what happened to her afterward – I thought a book could be written there. And only years later, when I was working at the *Sunday Times*, I went into the big hidden libraries in the Gray's Inn Road and said to the curator, "I sometimes thought I'd like to write a book about Lily..." but he said, "I can't tell you how many people I've told not to do that," and then he paused and looked at me, and I had published my book on Mary Woolstencraft at that time, and he said, "I think you might be the person to do it." So that was trying to show something that had been sort of hidden, really. The impetus of writing about Mary Woolstencraft was just a bit before that, which was that I happened to be reading her letters in the London Library and I thought, "This is an amazing woman" – she was there in the 1790s in London living a life very like my life (laughs) and I wanted to discover more about her so I went to Paris... I was just intensely curious. If you're very curious about a subject then you sit down to write about it. You want to make other people interested. And so it went on.

# THE WOMEN WRITERS' HANDBOOK

Q. When you are embarking on the biography of somebody, how soon do you have an idea of what you want the focus of the book to be, whether it's a personal event like the death of Hardy's wife, or later in the process when you've been through lots of other material?

A. I think you make great files, which used to be on paper and now on computer and you note down ... you have files and files of ideas and possibilities of starting and that sort of thing, and gradually you come to think "Well, this is the way to do it, this is the way I'd like to do it." I mean I did feel very strongly with Hardy that he always felt that he was primarily a poet but he has tended to be remembered as a novelist, for he wrote terrific novels, but I agree that his greatness is as a poet, starting in 1912 with the poems about his Emma, which are probably his greatest poems. It seems like a good way of doing it, but these are all arbitrary decisions that the writers make, of course.

Q. And have you found any difference between the research or the writing of a book about a female subject compared to a book about a male subject?

A. Not really, because in all cases there are a lot of characters of both sexes. I did enormously enjoy those early books I wrote about women, and very much enjoyed writing about Jane Austen because I had always read her books and I had read them with my daughters and discussed them, so it was a big pleasure, and also I found it quite exciting. It seemed to me that aspects of Jane Austen had been presented as a rather "posh" person and of course she wasn't – things like that.

Q. If you have a subject for whom there is a huge amount of archival material, how do you deal with that? Do you have a system or approach?

A. I'm dealing with that problem at the moment. Well, you just do your best, you scramble on, you try and cover the field. You know, I'm a reader, books are my life and I enjoy research very much.

Q. How hard was the decision to write your own autobiography?

## WOMEN'S VOICES

A. Well, I sometimes think perhaps I shouldn't have done it, I don't know quite why I did now. I suppose because I thought, getting into my mid-eighties, I would like to sort a few things out and because I had written about Pepys and so much admired Pepys's presentation of himself that he really was prepared to tell you pretty much everything about himself and I thought that made him so interesting, that made the world he lived in come to life and I thought, well, I've lived through an extraordinary period for women – when I went up to college hardly three per cent of women, I think, went to university in England. The 60s were so extraordinary and I thought, looking back, how I always thought I was making my own decisions but, in fact, I was often just being carried along with the tide of doing what other people were doing, and I got very interested in thinking about that and finding evidence of my own life in that. So I got interested enough to do it and to finish it. Of course you can't put everything in, and I think maybe some people have felt I shouldn't have done it, I don't know.

**Q. What would you say you wanted readers to take away?**

A. In the case of my books about women I really wanted to bring women forward as historical figures. I especially wanted to try and bring to life the people whom I write about. What could make them clearer on the page so that people feel they are really meeting them and hearing the voice as they read your book?

**Q. Can you identify a really good piece of advice you received as a writer?**

A. If you're trying to write and you feel you can't get started it's alright to say to yourself: "I'm writing a letter to a friend." And write whatever you might say in writing a letter to a friend and that will get you going. I can't say I've actually done that but I think it's terribly good advice. It really is also a good way of releasing you from a block. The advice I always want to give to people. is: "Just do it." What you have to do is have that blank page or that iPad sitting in front of you and you've just got to get on with it. I have to give advice to myself sometimes by getting up at six in the morning and working before breakfast. It's very good. That is very nice.

## THE WOMEN WRITERS' HANDBOOK

Q. Is there anything that you don't enjoy about the profession?

A. Well, it's very hard work at 86, I have to say. I work most of the time and I get very tired of it. It's very bad for any social life. I mean, you become very isolated. Because it's very hard to see friends and just do all those things you might like to do.

I'm writing a short book about the young H.G. Wells. I've always admired H.G. Wells and his formation story came from a poor background. He had a tremendous struggle and he had very bad health. Many interesting things about his formation. I'm going to go up to about age 40 and it is a huge amount of work.

And it is just completely fascinating. This is a very complicated person. He was so close with the Russians. He was a real socialist. He really wanted revolution. He was a Republican. He remained a Republican all his life. He's a most admirable figure but also very badly behaved in many ways – with women of course. He was prolific. His books like *The Time Machine* or *The War of the Worlds* have never been out of print since coming out in the 1880s. Isn't that extraordinary? Very few writers have success like that. When he was young he would write and publish about three books a year. It's hard to imagine how he did it.

Q. Have you noticed a change in reading tastes, or what the public is reading, over your lifetime?

A. I suppose. When I was sort of a young to middle-aged woman there were English novelists like Iris Murdoch or Kingsley Amis and when their books came out I absolutely had to have one that day. You felt there was a kind of momentum. American literature has changed things. We have a much broader range of reading, I think. When I was young too, if you were educated it was generally assumed you'd read French. Now we're getting some cross letters from readers who say "Oh you're assuming we know French!" and they quite rightly castigate us for that.

Q. What's the best decision you made in your professional career as a writer? And is there any decision that you regret?

A. Well I think I was right to accept being Literary Editor of *The New Statesman* after my husband was killed which was a difficult thing because

## WOMEN'S VOICES

I had four children. I talked about it with other friends and family. And you know some people thought I shouldn't do it. But I think I was right. I thought it was more interesting for my children to have a mother who is in the world working. I will say it was a completely fascinating job of course. I mean I had a job where the books come on your desk every day – it was like heaven. So I think that was a good decision.

Then I made the decision to give up and leave so I was able to devote myself to writing. But I made some stupid decisions. I mean I left at that stage because I'd had a success and had the commission for another book and I thought I could live on writing books but of course I couldn't write. I had to go back to being a mother.

Q. What's a typical day like when you're writing?

A. I might write in the morning then have lunch with my husband then in the afternoon I try and get back to work. It's very, very boring. My husband likes having people to lunch often. We sometimes walk by the river or go into Richmond. We go to the usual restaurants. That's it really.


### Claire Tomalin

After graduating from Newnham College, Cambridge, Claire Tomalin worked in publishing before becoming Literary Editor of both *New Statesman* magazine and the *Sunday Times* newspaper.

Her first book, *The Life and Death of Mary Wollstonecraft*, won the Whitbread First Book Award, and she has since written a number of highly acclaimed and bestselling biographies. They include *Jane Austen: A Life*, *The Invisible Woman*, a definitive account of Dickens' relationship with the actress Ellen Ternan, which won three major literary awards, and *Samuel Pepys: The Unequalled Self* was Whitbread Book of the Year in 2002. Her biography *Charles Dickens: A Life* provides an in-depth biography of the author. She is a trustee of the National Portrait Gallery, London and the Wordsworth Trust, a Fellow of the Royal Society of Literature and a Vice-President of English PEN.

She is married to the writer Michael Frayn.

Artwork by Selina Tusitala Marsh

# FORTUNE

## Ida Vitale
translated by Tanya Huntington

For years, to have enjoyed both the error
and its mending,
to have been able to speak and walk freely,
and existed without mutilation,
and entered churches, or not,
and read, heard music that is dear to me,
to have been at night a being, as in the light of day.
Not to have been married in a transaction
measured by goats,
not to have endured being governed by relatives,
or legal lapidation.
Never to have to march again
or ever condone words
that sow filaments of iron
in the bloodstream.
To discover on your own
another being, unforeseen
over the bridge of your gaze.
To be human and a woman, no more, no less.

## THE WOMEN WRITERS' HANDBOOK

*This poem was originally published in Literal Magazine. www.literalmagazine.com*

**Ida Vitale**

Ida Vitale was born in Montevideo, Uruguay in 1923. She is a literary critic, translator and author of more than a dozen poetry collections, including *La luz de esta memoria* (*The Light of this Remembrance*) (1949), *Palabra dada* (*Expectant Words*) (1953), *Cada uno en su noche* (*Each in His Own Night*) (1960), *Jardín de sílice* (*Garden of Silica*) (1978), *Procura de lo imposible* (*Procurement of the Impossible*) (1998), *Reducción del infinito* (*Reduction of the Infinite*) (2002), *El Abc de Byobú* (*Byobú's ABC*) (2005) and most recently *Plantas y animales* (*Plants and Animals*) (2003). Vitale is the recipient of international literary prizes such as the Octavio Paz Prize for Poetry and Essay (2009), the Alfonso Reyes International Prize (2015), the Reina Sofía Prize for Ibero-American Poetry (2015) and the Cervantes Prize. Vitale collaborated closely with Latin American literary magazines such as *Asir, Clinamen, Época, Jaque, Maldoror, Marcha, Uno más uno* and *Vuelta*. In 1973, she and her husband, the poet Enrique Fierro, sought exile in Mexico, where they lived until 1984. In 1989 they moved to Austin, Texas. Vitale now lives in Montevideo, Uruguay.

**Tanya Huntington**

Tanya Huntington is a bi-national writer and artist and the Managing Editor of the digital magazine *Literal: Latin American Voices*. Her most recent books are *Vidas sin fronteras* (Alfaguara Infantil, 2019) as an illustrator and *Solastalgia* (Almadía/UAA, 2018) as a poet. She holds a Ph.D. in Latin American Literature from the University of Maryland at College Park and currently teaches at CENTRO in Mexico City. She is a member of the National System of Creative Artists of the National Fund for Culture and the Arts (FONCA). @TanyaHuntington

# INTERVIEW WITH SARAH WATERS

Q. Who are your favourite women writers?

A. Rebecca West, Sylvia Townsend Warner, Patricia Highsmith, Muriel Spark, Angela Carter, Hilary Mantel and Shirley Hazzard.

Q. Which women writers inspired you?

A. Daphne du Maurier, Angela Carter, Patricia Highsmith and Philippa Gregory.

Q. Who helped you in your career?

A. Many people have helped me: supportive friends; fellow authors; excellent editors and publicists at my publishers in the UK and abroad; my fantastic partner, Lucy, who gives brutally honest feedback on my novels-in-progress; and above all my agent, Judith Murray. I've been with her from the very beginning, and she's been the one absolute constant in my writing career, an indefatigable source of wisdom, advice and encouragement.

Q. What do you enjoy most about being a writer?

The satisfaction of seeing a book through from the merest glimmer of a creative idea to the point where it exists in the world and can be read, enjoyed and reflected upon by other people.

Q. Is there anything you don't enjoy about being a writer?

A. Well, the writing process is full of highs and lows, and while the highs can be wonderful – cracking a problem, getting it right, feeling inspired, fizzing with excitement – the lows can be awful: exhaustion, lost confidence, loneliness, fear of failure... Also, on a practical level, my joints are full of aches and pains, after years of sitting twisted up at a computer for so many hours each day. (Advice to any would-be author:

invest in a really good ergonomic desk and chair; and take up pilates or yoga.)

**Q. What's the best piece of professional advice you were given?**

A. A friend who's always been a great, critical reader of my manuscripts said to me, early on, when I was feeling frustrated with a book-in-progress: "It would be a miracle if you got it right first time." How right she was, and I always keep that in mind. Writing is not really about writing at all – it's about patient re-writing.

**Q. What do you want readers to take away from your work?**

A. I'd like readers to finish a book of mine feeling entertained, moved and thoughtful.

**Q. What motivates you to write?**

A. I'm happiest when I'm writing – even if the book I'm working on seems full of unsolvable problems and is making me distinctly unhappy. Without a writing project, I feel lost – unmoored.

**Q. Do you have a favourite quotation from a book, poem, play or screenplay?**

A. I've always loved these lines from *Great Expectations*, which come at the end of the chapter in which Pip first meets Miss Havisham and Estella and has his life nudged on to a new path: "But, it is the same with any life. Imagine one selected day struck out of it, and think how different its course would have been. Pause you who read this, and think for a moment of the long chain of iron or gold, of thorns or flowers, that would never have bound you, but for the formation of the first link on one memorable day." A century and a half after Dickens wrote this, it's impossible not to do as his narrator commands and reflect on the significant encounters in our own lives. But this is also what writing fiction is all about, isn't it? Identifying the fateful moment; tracing the convoluted chains of iron, gold, thorns, flowers between one character and another.

**Q. How much of your own experience informs your writing?**

A. A lot – how could it not? But I don't think much of it would be recognizable to anyone else. It might make the clay of a novel but the clay is worked by the writing into brand new shapes.

## WOMEN'S VOICES

**Q. What do you think about the argument that writers should only write material based on their own cultural background?**

A. I think it's certainly true that writers need to be sensitive when they are using material that comes from cultures very distinct from their own – especially when they are writing about (and making money from) experiences that belong predominantly to people whose stories and voices have traditionally been muffled or misrepresented. But it would be sad, and reductive, if we could only draw on our own personal cultural backgrounds in our work. It's the very essence of writing, and reading, that we make an empathetic leap into someone else's point of view.

**Q. Do you think there has been any shift in reading/viewing tastes over your lifetime?**

A. In both commercial and literary fiction, and in film and TV, there's been a challenging of elites. We're less interested in reading stories from the mainstream than we are in reading stories from the margins. We want to hear from servants rather than from masters, from monsters rather than from heroes, from history's so-called losers rather than from its winners. This has made fiction much the richer, I think.

**Q. How do you anticipate reading/viewing tastes will change in future?**

A. I think books will get shorter, as our attention spans shrink! This is no bad thing. Most novels, it seems to me, could stand to lose a few pounds, especially ones by new writers, which tend to be a bit undisciplined. It's a great question to ask of your own manuscript: how much could this novel be pruned and yet still remain itself? Imagining your book as a screenplay is sometimes useful, because screenplays have to be lean and economical: they have to find the nub of a scene, and bring it to life in just a few lines of dialogue.

**Q. How conscious of genre are you when you write?**

A. It depends on the particular project I'm working on. All my books are historical novels, but they've engaged with history and with genre in different ways. *The Night Watch*, for example, is set in London during and just after the Second World War: I drew a lot on sources like diaries and letters, and saw the novel as intersecting more with social history than with genre. But with *Fingersmith*, say, or *The Little Stranger*, I really wanted to take on genre and have fun with it, bend it about a bit. *The Little Stranger* is a ghost story – a genre I've always loved – so it was a great treat to be able to give nods to the Gothic tradition in that novel, while also trying to take the genre into slightly new territory.

**Q. What are you most proud of?**

**A.** Lots of my lesbian readers tell me that some of my books – especially *Tipping the Velvet* and *Fingersmith* – have been really important to them, for example when they were young, or figuring out their sexuality, or trying to get over hurtful break-ups. That's not something I anticipated when I wrote those novels; I just wanted to write honestly about lesbian love. But it feels like an enormous privilege to have had an impact on people's emotional lives like that.

**Q. What's the best decision you've made in your writing career?**

**A.** To start it in the first place! I had an idea for a novel, but I had never written fiction before, so beginning to write creatively was a complete leap into the dark. But discovering how to do it – how to do the research, how to turn ideas into fiction, how to put together paragraphs, scenes, chapters – was enormously exciting and rewarding.

**Q. Have technological advances changed the way you write, or the way you are read/viewed?**

A. The way my novels are read has changed a lot, in that people can now access them on e-readers, on tablets and phones, and as audio books. The way I do my research has changed too: when I started off, twenty-five years ago, I was pretty much limited to books. If I wanted to find out, say, what a theatrical dressing room looked like in the 1890s, I would have to go to a specialist library, possibly order a book from a catalogue and wait for it to arrive. Now I can find the same information, online, in an instant. That's a pretty amazing change. (It's almost too useful, at times: it's possible to look at image after image, going from one website to another, for hours at a time.) But my day-to-day writing life hasn't changed at all, and is still very low-tech. I just need a desk, a chair and a computer for the actual composing, and, for the editing – because I like to edit drafts by hand – a printer, some paper and a couple of coloured pens.

## WOMEN'S VOICES

**Q. Do you engage with readers via festivals, talks or social media?**

A. I don't use social media, but I always reply to the emails and letters that are passed on to me from readers by my publisher, and I really love meeting readers at talks and festivals – it's absolutely the best part of the event.

**Q. What advice would you give to a new writer?**

A. Put the hours in. It's no good waiting for inspiration to strike, because it probably won't. You have to turn up at your desk for work, day after day, week after week, month after month, year after year. You have to get something down on paper – and then you have to be prepared to rewrite it, possibly many times, because your first few drafts will almost certainly not be very good. You have to be willing to write rubbish, and then figure out how to make it better. It's hard! But it will be fantastically satisfying when you get there in the end.


**Sarah Waters**

Sarah Waters was born in Wales. She is the author of six novels, *Tipping the Velvet, Affinity, Fingersmith, The Night Watch, The Little Stranger* and *The Paying Guests*, which have been adapted for stage, television and feature film in the UK and US. Her novels have been shortlisted for the Man Booker Prize and the Women's Prize for Fiction and she has won the Betty Trask Award, the Somerset Maugham Award, The *Sunday Times* Young Writer of the Year Award, the South Bank Show Award for Literature and the CWA Historical Dagger. She has been named Author of the Year four times: by the British Book Awards, the Booksellers' Association, Waterstones Booksellers, Stonewall's Writer of the Decade in 2015, *Diva* Magazine Author of the Year Award and The *Sunday Times* Award for Literary Excellence in 2017, which is given in recognition of a writer's entire body of work. Waters was awarded an OBE in 2019 for services to literature in the Queen's Birthday Honours. She lives in London.

"*You can always edit a bad page. You can't edit a blank page.*"
— Jodi Picoult

# VIRGINIA WOOLF, 100 YEARS ON...

## Emma Woolf

One hundred years ago, with the publication of *Night and Day* in 1919, Virginia Woolf was beginning to gain literary recognition. However, her private life was more troubled. As her great-niece, I thought it would be interesting to re-examine her letters and diaries to understand why those early years of her career were so turbulent for the writer, and what role her marriage, Bloomsbury and the First World War played in her recurrent breakdowns.

"I caused some slight argument with Leonard this morning by trying to cook my breakfast in bed. I believe, however, that the good sense of the proceeding will make it prevail; that is, if I can dispose of the eggshells..."

So wrote Virginia Woolf in January 1915, musing on her latest domestic experiment. This attempt to cook eggs in bed was a lighter interlude in what was to become one of the worst years of her life. Reading her letters and diaries recently in the London Library, I discovered a more playful side to the modernist writer we have come to think of as stern, humourless, even tortured. Virginia's daily journal and correspondence reveal a sensitive, perceptive young woman who loved a "debauch of gossip" with her friends. That diary entry from early 1915 was a precious lull before the storm: one month later she plunged into a nervous breakdown so severe that she lost the rest of the year.

Sadly, these breakdowns were nothing new. The sudden death of her mother from rheumatic fever in 1895 had provoked Virginia's first breakdown at the age of 13. Her father's death in 1904 triggered her

## THE WOMEN WRITERS' HANDBOOK

second collapse; her nephew and biographer Quentin Bell wrote: "All that summer she was mad." She also endured the death of her half-sister Stella in 1897 and her beloved brother Thoby in 1907; the repeated bereavements took their toll on her mental health. Virginia's third breakdown in 1913, aged 31, occurred less than a year after her marriage to Leonard Woolf.

During the course of 1913–15 she made several suicide attempts, including trying to jump from a window and overdosing on Veronal, a powerful sedative. As the "madness" took hold, she stopped eating or sleeping, and at times she hallucinated – Quentin Bell records that she once heard "the birds singing in Greek and [imagined] that King Edward VII lurked in the azaleas using the foulest possible language".

And yet this ought to have been a happy period for Virginia. As well as the publication of her first novel (*The Voyage Out* in 1915), she was starting to make a living from reviewing and other critical writing. She and Leonard were living in Richmond, a leafy suburb of London, making plans to set up their own printing press (and even contemplating buying a bulldog they wanted to call John). So why did she become so unwell?

She had been grappling with endless drafts of *The Voyage Out* for four or five years – Leonard recalled her rewriting it "with a kind of tortured intensity". It was finally published on 26th March 1915, the day after Virginia entered the nursing home where she was to remain for the next six months. The novel had been accepted for publication in 1913 (by her half-brother Gerald Duckworth, who is said to have sexually abused her as a child) but delayed because of her hospitalization. Throughout Virginia's life, the process of completing a book and working on proofs was a time of extreme anxiety, followed by the terrible wait for publication, and, still worse, the critical response. In 1936, while struggling with *The Years*, she recalled the misery and self-doubt she had experienced two decades earlier: "I have never suffered, since *The Voyage Out*, such acute despair on re reading... Never been so near the precipice to my own feeling since 1913."

It was appropriate that I was rediscovering my great-aunt's letters and diaries in the London Library: her father Sir Leslie Stephen was President of the Library from 1892 until his death in 1904. Virginia referred to it as "a stale culture smoked place" in 1915, although she was a regular visitor. When a librarian recently showed me her original registration form, I was moved to see that she joined the library four days after her father's death. (Despite being only 22 years old, she describes her occupation on the form as "spinster".)

The joy of Virginia's personal writings is the lively and varied content, from literary highs to domestic lows, gossip about her contemporaries and relatives, often satirical, sometimes spiteful (especially about the "Jews", Leonard's large family). On the one hand she is writing to the poet Thomas Hardy: "I have long wished to tell you how profoundly grateful I am to you for your poems and novels, but naturally it seemed an impertinence to do so." (17th Jan 1915). And in her diary at the same time she is documenting the daily catastrophes in their "House of Trouble" in Richmond: on a typical January day "the pipes burst; or got choked; or the roof split asunder. Anyhow in the middle of the morning, I heard a steady rush of water in the wainscot… various people have been clambering about the roof ever since. The water still drips through the ceiling into a row of slop pails."

The diaries also offer a fascinating insight into Virginia's early development as a writer: "I wrote all the morning, with infinite pleasure, which is queer, because I know all the time that there is no reason to be pleased with what I write, and that in 6 weeks or even days, I shall hate it." (6th January 1915.) These sound like the typical ups and downs of any writer, not a woman on the verge of a nervous breakdown.

According to those closest to Virginia, particularly Leonard and her sister Vanessa Bell, completing *The Voyage Out* was a factor in her 1915 breakdown. So, what was in the novel to trigger such a collapse? There are many interesting parallels between the novel and Virginia's own life during the years she was writing it. Her heroine Rachel Vinrace, on a sea-voyage from England to the sultry South American jungle, is also on a journey of self-discovery; this journey mirrors Virginia's own transition from sheltered Victorian childhood in South Kensington to the intellectual and sexual liberation of Bloomsbury (where she moved with her siblings following their father's death in 1904). Similarly, Rachel's first steps into womanhood are echoed in Virginia's personal development: while rewriting *The Voyage Out* she would become engaged and then married to Leonard Woolf. Virginity, violation and fear of sexual intimacy are constant, uneasy themes in the novel, reflecting the anxieties of both heroine and author.

Hesitating throughout the spring of 1912 over Leonard's proposal, Virginia struggled to reconcile "being half in love" with him with a sort of revulsion over "the sexual side of it". Writing to him a few weeks before they became engaged, she explained what was holding her back: "As I told you brutally the other day, I feel no attraction in you. There are moments – when you kissed me the other day was one – when I feel no more than a rock." She hesitated not because she felt too little, but perhaps because she hoped for too much. "We both of us want a marriage that is a tremendous living thing, always alive, always hot, not dead and easy in parts as most marriages are. We ask a great deal of life, don't we?" (May 1912).

Her heroine Rachel Vinrace expresses similar sentiments, telling her prospective husband Terence Hewet: "I've cared for heaps of people, but not to marry them… All my life I've wanted somebody I could look up to, somebody great and big and splendid. Most men are so small." Like Virginia, Rachel admires her future husband, but she is also apprehensive about what is expected of her as a wife. Shortly after Rachel accepts Terence she plunges into the tropical fever which will kill her. She suffers disturbing hallucinations: "While all her tormentors thought that she was dead, she was not dead, but curled up at the bottom of the sea." Virginia writes to Leonard: "I feel angry sometimes at the strength of your desire," and Rachel says of male sexual desire: "It is terrifying – it is disgusting." Whether or not Virginia had been sexually abused as a child, it's no wonder that writing and rewriting *The Voyage Out* exacerbated her instability in the years leading up to its publication.

There has been much speculation about the sexual dimension of the Woolfs' relationship: was the marriage even consummated, was she frigid, was she a lesbian? In 1967 Gerald Brenan added fuel to the fire, writing: "Leonard told me that when on their honeymoon he had tried to make love to her she had got into such a violent state of excitement that he had had to stop, knowing as he did that these states were a prelude to her attacks of madness… So Leonard had to give up all idea of ever having any sort of sexual satisfaction."

## WOMEN'S VOICES

Can this be true? What did Virginia expect from their marriage? Before their engagement she wrote to Leonard: "I want everything – love, children, adventure, intimacy, work." She is often portrayed as unmaternal, but this seems inaccurate. She adored looking after her sister Vanessa's children, and she and Leonard hoped for a family of their own, as this poignant letter in 1913 reveals: "We aren't going to have a baby, but we want to have one..." For me, one of the saddest insights in Virginia's letters and diaries is the profound sense of loss for the family they never had. She blamed herself for their childlessness, writing to a friend in 1926: "A little more self-control on my part, and we might have had a boy of 12, a girl of 10."

However, it had been decided (by Leonard, Vanessa and her doctors) that she was too unstable for motherhood – as her sister interferingly wrote: "the risk she runs is that of another bad nervous breakdown, and I doubt if even a baby would be worth that." (Given that not having children did not prevent her breakdowns, one wonders whether it might have helped.)

During 1910, 1912 and 1913 Virginia was sent for rest cures in Twickenham to "a private nursing home for women with nervous disorder". As well as enforced seclusion, she was placed on a regime of weight gain; four or five pints of milk daily, as well as cutlets, liquid malt extract and beef tea. The recommendation from her psychiatrist was that a patient "who went in weighing seven stone six comes out weighing 12". This advice clearly made an impact on Virginia: she repeats it almost verbatim in *Mrs Dalloway* (1925), when the celebrated psychiatrist Sir William Bradshaw orders "rest in bed; rest in solitude; silence and rest; rest without books... so that a patient who went in weighing seven stone six comes out weighing twelve".

Understandably, Virginia felt frustrated at being infantilized in this way, with all her decisions made for her. In 1912 she complained: "Leonard made me into a comatose invalid." This accusation is not without a degree of truth: he replaced the excitement and social whirl of Bloomsbury with the relative quiet of Richmond, he made her spend the mornings in bed, he monitored her eating and weight, her moods and menstrual cycles.

His insistence on rest and rich food continued throughout her life: shortly before her suicide in 1941, Virginia rages impotently in a letter to her doctor about "the cream, the cheese, the milk". However, she also knew that Leonard was right about the "danger signals". As she wrote to Jacques Raverat in 1922, "unless I weigh 9 and half stones I hear voices and see visions and can neither write nor sleep". And she knew that she owed Leonard her life, as she wrote in 1929 to her reputed lover Vita Sackville-West: "I should have shot myself long ago in one of these illnesses if it hadn't been for him."

Her doctors insisted on "total rest of the intellect", so there are gaps in Virginia's letters and diaries during the "mad" times. Fortunately Leonard, a former colonial civil servant, was a meticulous note-taker; his autobiography, *Beginning Again* (1911–1918) sheds much light on how and why her crises unfolded. It wasn't only Virginia's health that he documented; my father recalled working lunches with his uncle: "He went to the nearest bakery and bought two penny bread rolls and butter and sat on a park bench. He took out a black covered notebook and wrote down, 'Two bread rolls. 2 pence.' Everything was recorded. He recorded the score at bowls; he recorded the yield of every fruit tree in the garden." Another time, my father recalls T.S. Eliot saying: "Leonard invited me to lunch at Victoria Square, and all he gave me was a bag of chips and a bottle of ginger beer." In fact Leonard wasn't mean, just very careful with money – a character trait made famous by Virginia's announcement of their engagement: "I'm to marry a penniless Jew."

Comments like this, probably meant affectionately, have earned her the reputation of being snobbish, even anti-semitic. But what was Virginia really like? My father Cecil Woolf (who lived in Leonard's London home for 30 years) remembers his aunt as: "volatile, mercurial, moody... She could be quite sharp – she looked sharp, her face was sharp. When you arrived at their house, she would ask you about your journey and she wanted every detail. 'Okay, you came by train. Tell me about the people in the carriage,' she'd probe... It was the novelist's search for copy, ideas. Leonard referred to this as 'Virginia taking off'."

My father recalls how she would recycle information: "You'd tell her something, a little story or an account, and the next week she would have built it into a big deal, exaggerating everything. By the time she'd finished

## WOMEN'S VOICES

the fictionalisation of an incident, it could be amusing but it could also be embarrassing for the person at the centre of things."

\*

If those early decades of the 20th century were troubled for the Woolfs, Europe was also in turmoil. Although Virginia does not write directly about war, the conflict resonates through her novels, particularly *Jacob's Room* (1922) and *Mrs Dalloway* (1925), with their legacy of loss, shell-shock and a generation changed forever. The recurrent symbols of distant armies, bombs and guns overheard across the Channel in *To The Lighthouse* (1927) and *The Years* (1937) also have their origins in the First World War.

In January 1915 German strategic bombing had begun, with zeppelin raids over London. Most of Virginia's Bloomsbury social set were vehemently anti-war, including Maynard Keynes, Lytton Strachey – and Leonard, who thought the war was "senseless and useless". Her brother-in-law Clive Bell's anti-war pamphlet was destroyed by the Lord Mayor of London, and her friend Bertrand Russell was imprisoned for pacifism. When conscription was introduced in 1916, Virginia wrote to a friend: "The whole of our world does nothing but talk about conscription, and their chances of getting off." Leonard did "get off", due to his shaking hands (a hereditary tremor) and his wife's mental instability.

Virginia's opposition to war was closely linked to her feminism: she described it as a "preposterous masculine fiction", and yet another outcome of male chauvinism. She wrote in *Three Guineas* (1938) that "the chief occupations of men are the shedding of blood, the making of money, the giving of orders, and the wearing of uniforms..."

The war features frequently in the wartime letters and diaries as a practical inconvenience as well as an ideological question (she would, after all, spend many nights sheltering in the cellar of Hogarth House). In January 1915 she refers to that "queer winter – the worst I ever knew, and suitable for the war and all the rest of it". References to food rationing and shortages are mixed with newspaper headlines of naval victory: "we have sunk a German battle ship". And in November 1917 at the Battle of Cambrai, a single shell killed one of Leonard's brothers (Cecil) and wounded the other (Philip, my grandfather).

## THE WOMEN WRITERS' HANDBOOK

Hating the war, Virginia also detested the popular "Hang the Kaiser" jingoism of her compatriots, writing in January 1915 to the artist Duncan Grant: "they seem full of the most violent and filthy passions." In the same letter she mentions a Queens Hall concert "where the patriotic sentiment was so revolting that I was nearly sick".

Despite the mounting casualties, and Virginia's uncertain health, there were intensely happy times too. Her 33rd birthday, for example, when Leonard "crept into my bed, with a little parcel, which was a beautiful green purse... I was then taken up to town, free of charge, and given a treat, first at a Picture Palace, and then at Buszards [tearooms in Oxford St]... I don't know when I have enjoyed a birthday so much..." (January 25th, 1915)

Many diary entries of this time are positively carefree. Virginia describes a shopping trip after her skirt has split in two: Leonard goes to the library and she to "ramble about the West End, picking up clothes. I am really in rags. It is very amusing... I bought a ten and elevenpenny blue dress." She muses on how London inspires her writing: "I had tea, and rambled down to Charing Cross in the dark, making up phrases and incidents to write about. Which is, I expect, the way one gets killed." (February 1915). Two days later they went to see a printing press in Farringdon – delayed by Virginia's illness, they would finally set up the Hogarth Press in 1917, publishing T.S. Eliot, Katherine Mansfield, E.M. Forster and Sigmund Freud, among many notable 20th century authors.

On 23rd February Virginia suddenly became incoherent. Her letters a few days later refer to this brief attack: "I am now all right though rather tired"; "I am now well again and it is very wonderful"; "I have to keep lying down, but I am getting better".

In fact, Virginia's health deteriorated further. At the end of February 1915 she "entered a state of garrulous mania, speaking ever more wildly, incoherently and incessantly, until she lapsed into gibberish and sank into a coma" (Quentin Bell). By March she was being cared for by professional nurses, and was unable to see or speak to Leonard he writes that she was "violently hostile". At times her psychotic episodes were so severe that she required four nurses to hold her down, and there was genuine doubt over whether she would ever fully recover. She remained under professional care until November 1915, when she finally returned to Hogarth House: "I spend my spare time in bed, but I'm allowed out in the afternoons, and thank God the last Nurse is gone."

Whatever the truth about their marriage, it was a partnership of great importance to 20th century literature. Without Leonard it's unlikely that Virginia would have survived her suicide attempts of 1913–1915, let alone stayed alive long enough to write *Mrs Dalloway*, *To The Lighthouse* or *The Waves*, now considered seminal modernist texts.

And there is no doubting the profound love between them. Virginia's suicide note to Leonard, written before she drowned herself in the River Ouse in March 1941, is testament to that extraordinary closeness: "What I want to say is I owe all the happiness of my life to you. You have been entirely patient with me and incredibly good... I don't think two people could have been happier than we have been." This farewell is hauntingly foreshadowed by Terence's final words to Rachel on her deathbed, written thirty years before: "No two people have ever been so happy as we have been..."

When *The Voyage Out* was published, just over 100 years ago, it was well received by the critics, although by then Virginia was too ill to know. Nor was she present when Leonard formally registered her as an "author" a few days later. In January 1915, after a walk along the River Thames (with her dog getting into a fight, and her suspenders coming down) she had noted in her diary: "My writing now delights me solely because I love writing and don't, honestly, care a hang what anyone says. What seas of horror one dives through in order to pick up these pearls – however they are worth it."

In the end, Virginia's madness was part of the writing, and the writing was part of the madness. Perhaps the seas of horror were worth it for the pearls.

# THE WOMEN WRITERS' HANDBOOK

**Emma Woolf**

Emma Woolf is a writer, journalist and broadcaster. Born in London, she studied English at Oxford University. She worked in psychology publishing before becoming a columnist for The *Times* and *Newsweek*, TV presenter on Channel 4 and commentator across the BBC. She is a reviewer and arts critic for Radio 4 and Radio 5 Live and speaks internationally at literary festivals from Cheltenham to Mumbai. Emma's books have been translated around the world, including the bestselling: *An Apple a Day: A Memoir of Love & Recovery from Anorexia* (2012), *The Ministry of Thin: How The Pursuit of Perfection Got Out of Control* (2013), *Ways of Escape* (2014), *Letting Go: Heal Your Hurt, Love Your Body & Transform Your Life* (2015), *Positively Primal: Finding Health & Happiness in a Hectic World* (2016), *The A-Z of Eating Disorders* (2017), *England's Lane* (2018), *Wellbeing: Body Confidence, Health & Happiness* (2019).

www.emmawoolf.com and @EJWoolf

*"But there is no gate, no lock, no bolt that you can set upon the freedom of my mind."*
— Virginia Woolf

Artwork by Susannah Felstead

# WRITING WORKSHOPS

In using the following exercises, it's important that each stage is negotiated with members of the group so that anything which may arise has time to be addressed. Workshop leaders can assess how much time to allow for each task depending on group size. By sharing the different ways in which we approach writing, an understanding of the process can be developed and support given to each writer at each stage of their journey.

Attending a writers' group for the first time and sharing your work out loud can be a nerve-wracking experience. As participants listen and value each other's work, an attitude of mutual trust and respect develops. Initial embarrassment soon passes and members are able to share personal, often intimate experiences, in a supportive and caring atmosphere. A lack of commitment from any group member, who is repeatedly late or never shares any of her own writing, can impact the group and a workshop leader is wise to address this early on.

Many women worry that there will never be enough time to share their work, others may feel guilty about taking up too much of the group's time. It's common for members to apologise for, or deride their own work before it is read out and discussed. The workshop leader ensures that there is enough time for each participant's writing to be shared and helps members present their work in a positive way.

Varying the group size according to the activity is important. Often a workshop will begin with whole group work to allow for the introduction of tasks and clarification of themes, then at the end, to give general feedback and for insights to be shared. Work in pairs allows a discussion of a more personal nature than whole group work and can create bonding among members. Working with different partners breaks down social barriers and encourages cohesion of the group.

**WRITING WORKSHOPS**

## Self-Assessment

**Aims: To evaluate what a writer needs and how to progress**

**Method:**
1. Each member of the group should take four sheets of paper. Give each page one of the following titles: Skills, Problems, Support Systems, Ambitions.
2. Under each title, list your own
a) Skills – talents, qualities, what you're good at.
b) Problems – obstacles, difficulties, worries.
c) Support systems – things that keep you going, stimulants, good friends, family etc.
d) Ambitions – hopes and dreams.
3. Study your lists and write down three conclusions about whether you are managing to use your skills to achieve your ambitions. If you find it hard to identify skills this may suggest a lack of confidence.

If you find you have few support systems, you may be unwilling to seek help with problems.

If you have the same thing on two lists, e.g. a relationship may be supportive and problematic, or alcohol might be a support system and a problem, try and draw some conclusion about future plans.

4. Discussion of the group's feelings about this exercise.

Note: This exercise is designed to help writers identify those areas which may prevent them from using their talents to the full.

Lists should be made privately to enable total honesty.

Writers can then raise personal issues they wish to address and choose which issues they bring to the group for discussion afterwards.

This exercise can be combined with any of the following exercises.

## Becoming A Writer

**Aim: To overcome internal fears and misgivings about being a writer.**

**Method:**

1. Place three chairs facing each other in the centre of the room. One chair is for the "Novice Writer", the second is for the "Struggling Writer" and the third is for the "Famous Writer."

*Notes on Roles:* the Novice is in awe of the Famous Writer and idealistic about her future career. The Struggling Writer is experienced but is not successful enough to work full-time as a writer and is considering giving it up. The Famous Writer has been extremely successful, but has ceased to have anything new to say.

2. Three volunteers take on these roles. They improvise meeting at a conference where they discuss their writing with each other.

3. At any time, the action can be stopped by the command "Freeze", and any other member of the group can swap into one of the roles and continue.

Note: This gives the participants the experience and status of being writers and the opportunity to air and discuss fears and anxieties which they may bring to the workshop. Problems like childcare, lack of confidence, money, education etc. can be shared as common difficulties and not as overwhelming obstacles to success.

4. Ask for feedback from participants about how they felt in each of the roles and what they learned from the experience.

*"Nothing, I believe, is so full of life under the microscope as a drop of water from a stagnant pool."*
— Agatha Christie

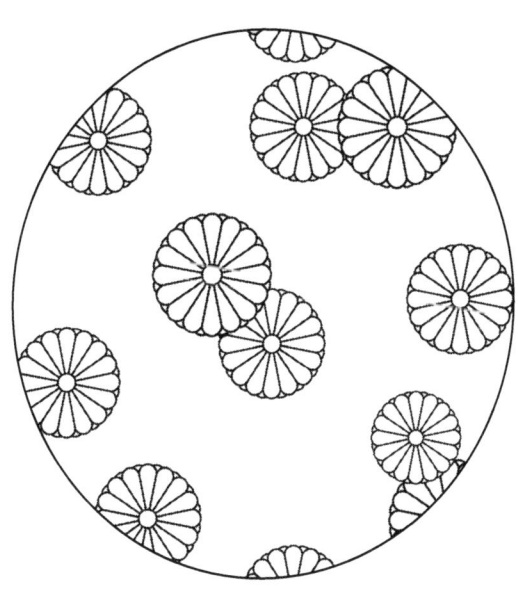

THE WOMEN WRITERS' HANDBOOK

# A Room of One's Own

Aim: To look at the ways we use our space and to explore a writer's need for mental space.

Method:
1. Brainstorm the word "Space" for association and write these on a large sheet in the centre of the room.

2. In pairs, describe your current room vividly – the colours, the smells, the sounds etc. Swap round.

3. Make a list of home improvements you'd like to make given an unlimited budget and share this list with your partner.

4. Think of a communal room in your present or past home and draw a picture from above of the way it is laid out.

5. Colour-code items and spaces in the room which are:
a) exclusively yours
b) shared ownership
c) never used by you

6. Discuss how much of the room is yours? Which parts are shared? Which parts are essential to you? Which parts are subject to conflict?

7. Imagine this conflict on a grander scale. Imagine a character who demands the right to a certain object or space. Write a story/poem/scene/monologue about this conflict.

8. Share and discuss. What space do you create for your writing?

9. Look back at the original associations for the word "Space". What other words might we add now?

**WRITING WORKSHOPS**

# Developing Complex Characters

**Aim: To deepen character.**

**Method:**
1. Discuss opposition and conflict in stories, in soaps, in recent plays.
2. Invent a character with an aim or mission in life.
3. Invent obstacles to this character's success on three levels:
a) Conflict with self
b) Conflict with family and friends
c) Conflict with society/authority/environment.
4. Invent situations in which the character will come into conflict on each of these three levels. The choices the character makes in these situations are often known as 'turning-points.'
5. What is the outcome of these choices? Do they lead to further complications and difficulties for the character to resolve before they can achieve their aim? Do they succeed too easily?
6. Make up a chart of the character's journey along the lines of a board-game (Snakes and Ladders/Monopoly). Draw in alternate choices for your character at each stage – the moves s/he doesn't make in your story, but could have made.
7. Choose one moment from your chart and hot-seat a member of the group who role-plays their character at that moment of the story.
8. Discuss this moment and what we learn about the character from it. Look at the character's chart. Does it bear out what we expect of them?
9. Repeat with other members of the group.
10. Write this scene, portraying the moment of choice for the character.
11. Share and discuss.

THE WOMEN WRITERS' HANDBOOK

# Clichés, Lies and Exaggerations

Aim: To examine use and over-use of language. To facilitate writing dialogue.

Method:
1. Introduction and discussion of examples of "bad" dialogue. What is wrong? e. g. Over-explaining/too much information; use of dated or unintelligible slang; irrelevant chat; attempt at "poetic" language; obvious statements; lack of subtext; failure to demonstrate character attitude or emotion.

2. In small groups, devise a short scene from a soap opera, real or imaginary, to demonstrate the use of bad dialogue.

3. Share these with the whole group and discuss.

4. In the same groups try to rework the scenes into effective dialogue.

5. Share, or read aloud and discuss. What hooks did they use to engage interest? e.g. questions, strong reactions, interruptions, repetitions, force of persuasion. Was the dialogue in keeping with what we already know about the character's background and personality? Was it clichéd?

6. Discuss clichés and hackneyed language. Should we avoid them? How can we use them to effect?

7. In pairs, make lists of the clichéd dialogue associated with the following situations: Doctors and patients / teacher and pupils / lovers in love / rejected lovers. etc.

8. Read out the lists and then join with another pair and read out alternate lines from each list so that a new scene is created. How easy is it to swap clichés from one scene to another? Do they work better in a different context? Discuss.

9. Write on a slip of paper a line of dialogue which defines an attitude such as "Never say die" or "Don't rock the boat."

10. Repeat with another slip of paper. Fold both slips and place them in a pile in the centre of the room.

11. Choose two different pieces of paper.

## WRITING WORKSHOPS

12. Two volunteers role-play a scene, which they devise by using one of the attitudes they have selected. Could we easily identify their character attitudes?

13. Write a short piece with two characters, using the two attitudes you have selected from the pile.

14. Share and discuss.

# THE WOMEN WRITERS' HANDBOOK

## Mothers/Fathers

**Aim:** To explore feelings and ideas about: motherhood; eg sacrifice/devotion/guilt/disapproval
or fatherhood; eg authority/success/social identity/tyranny

**Method:**

1. Draw a picture of an early memory of your mother /grandmother / a mother figure or father/grandfather/a father figure.

2. Think of three adjectives to describe this person and write them below the picture.

3. Share some of the adjectives with the group.

4. Divide into small groups to discuss and share memories. Some members may not feel able to do this unless they work in a pair with a trusted partner.

5. Each group chooses one person's memory to sculpt in the form of a frozen picture using the other group members.

6. Come together, and then the groups choose one by one to share their sculpted group pictures.

7. Each picture is given a title by the group.

8. Ask for one group to update their picture. Beginning with the first frozen picture positioning, the picture-maker moves and changes the elements to represent a more recent memory.

9. Discuss what changed, e.g. power relationships, relative size, body language, distance, attitudes etc. What did the pictures evoke for the audience and the participants?

10. Write a story/scene/poem/monologue about a mother or father.

11. Share and discuss.

12. Looking back at the pictures and adjectives, discuss how our relationships with mothers or fathers may affect our feelings towards other women or male authority, our attitudes to our careers, and our sense of self.

Note: can also substitute sisters or brothers

## WRITING WORKSHOPS

## Fear of Failure

Aim: To explore the fears we have about success and failure and to look at ways in which we sabotage ourselves and our work. To help build group cohesion.

Method:
1. a) In pairs, A tells B a problem about work/writing. B demonstrates non-verbally through "Body-Language" that she is not interested. Swap over.

b) Same pairs. This time, each partner expresses a great deal of concern and encouragement in acknowledging the other's problem.

2. Discuss these exercises and the ways in which people communicated their attitudes. What strategies were used to dismiss or encourage? How do we feel about positive/negative responses? Do we often receive a negative response which blocks us? Do we seek encouragement in the wrong places? How do we ensure we get the right response?

3. In groups of three, A and B hold an intimate conversation. Person C tries to interrupt, destroy, distract from the conversation A and B are having. When C has succeeded in steering the conversation in her own direction, stop and swap round.

4. Discuss the strategies that were used to sabotage the interaction between A and B. How did it feel being excluded? How easy was it to sabotage A and B?

5. In a circle, the whole group does a round of:

a) I could sabotage this group by ....

b) I could help this group by ...

c) I sabotage my work by ...

d) I could help my work by ...

6. A volunteer is asked to "mould" or "sculpt" a frozen picture/ tableau of a memory they have of an incident involving sabotage or self-sabotage. They use the other members of the group to create their picture.

## THE WOMEN WRITERS' HANDBOOK

7. The rest of the group walk round the picture and comment on what they see, offering titles for it. Members can swap in and out of the picture so that everyone can see it.

8. Discuss what thoughts and feelings were evoked. How much do we sabotage ourselves in our daily lives?

WRITING WORKSHOPS

# Self-Censorship

**Aim:** to identify and overcome a writer's personal block with/without a specific piece of work.

**Method:**

1. A volunteer takes a chair in the centre of the circle. The leader asks her to choose members of the group to 'act out' her blocks.

i.e. if the woman in the hotseat feels that a particular teacher at school, a parent, a sibling, or a favourite writer is getting in the way of her writing, she chooses another member of the group to represent each person she has mentioned (CENSORS).

2. Women playing the censors then stand around her and place their hands lightly on her shoulders, and the volunteer explains to them the inhibiting attitudes of the people they represent.

3. The volunteer then begins to talk about her current project, or her writing in general, or her feelings about being a writer. Each time she says anything that might offend/alienate/upset one of the censors, they press on her shoulder and she must ask them what she has said to offend them, and then argue against their censorship, convincing them to remove their hand and sit down.

4. The process continues until each censor has been confronted and has removed their pressure.

5. Discuss.

Note: A volunteer may choose censors for a variety of reasons: either, a friend/relative/colleague who specifically disparages her writing, or a favourite writer who is so good the volunteer feels that there is no point in competing (this is also a good exercise for establishing a personal voice).

– a family member whose attitudes are important to the woman, and who is discouraging, or who specifically/implicitly censors a certain subject area e.g. a parent may not like their daughter writing about her sexual experiences.

This exercise is adapted from a workshop given originally by Jules Wright. (WPT).

## THE WOMEN WRITERS' HANDBOOK

## Subverting Fairytales

Aim: To find alternate endings for age-old stories. To look at the way feminism has changed our perceptions.

Method:
1. Read the traditional story *The Little Mermaid*.
2. Read *The Pangs of Love* by Jane Gardam*.
3. Divide into two groups. Group A prepares an improvised scene from *The Little Mermaid*. Group B prepares an improvised scene from the *The Pangs of Love*.
4. Group A presents their scene once and Group B watch it with a view to adding a new soundtrack to it in line with their author's view of the world.
5. Group B discuss the new soundtrack and then ask Group A to re-run the scene silently. Group B provide the sounds effects, dialogue, music, narration etc.
6. Repeat with the scene Group B have prepared. This time group A devise a new soundtrack from the perspective of the Hans Christian Andersen original. Group B re-run the scene with the new soundtrack.
7. Discuss the effect of this counterpointing. Discuss how Jane Gardam changed the original. What kind of language/style/characterisation did she employ? Make a list of techniques that were used by the groups and the writer to subvert the original story, e.g. parody, bathos, exaggeration, repetition etc.
8. Choose a fairytale you know well.
9. Write a new version of it from a different perspective. Try using some of the techniques you have listed, try updating it or changing the setting.

What kind of ending do you want for your story?

10. Share these and discuss.

Note: For further reading about Fairytales see:

## WRITING WORKSHOPS

*The Pangs of Love and other stories* by Jane Gardam.
Also included in *Close Company* collection (Virago)
*The Uses of Enchantment* by Bruno Bettelheim.
*The Bloody Chamber* by Angela Carter.
*Women who run with the Wolves; myths and stories of the Wild Woman archetype*
Clarissa Pinkola Estés.

Artwork by Virginia Frances Sterrett

## Conflict / Violence

**Aim:** To explore a strong theme using drama techniques. To overcome avoidance of conflict in stories.

**Method:**
1. Draw a picture of an act of violence.
2. Describe it with three adjectives.
3. Take on the adjectives yourself in a round e.g. "I am violent", "I am arbitrary", "I am political", etc. Go round the group three times and hear all the adjectives.
4. In pairs, A takes on the role of aggressor, B the role of counsellor. A speaks about the act of violence he/she has committed against another, as if for the first time (in role), while B listens.
5. B reports back what she/he has been told, to the group. How difficult was it to take on the role of aggressor? Did you modify your original act of violence when asked to do this? Discuss.
6. In the same pairs A and B reverse roles. This time, recalling the original adjectives, B has been violent, but he/she is 'the victim' – not an outsider, and the act is more one of self-destruction. A takes on the role of counsellor hearing the story for the first time.
7. A reports back to the whole group. How were these stories different?

Was it easier to identify with the violence? What was the attitude of the self-destructive character to the self-inflicted violence? How did this compare with the attitudes of the aggressors in the preceding exercise? Discuss.

8. Choose to be either the aggressor or the victim. Write a piece about conflict or violence.
9. Share these and discuss.

## WRITING WORKSHOPS

# Voice

**Aim:** To listen and tell stories and to explore the idea of a writer's "voice".

**Method:**

1. In pairs: A thinks of a recent story (from the news, real life or imaginary).
2. A tells B his/her story. B listens and has to think of one word to describe how he/she feels, after hearing this story.
3. In the whole group, B reports back A's story and gives his/her one "word". The leader may ask supplementary questions such as: What effect did the story have on the listener? Did the reporter improve on the story? What was best about the story? How would you describe the way A told the story (ie the "voice")?
4. Discuss which stories were most effective. How much did the personality of the storyteller influence the listener? What made a story interesting? What made it boring?
5. Individually, choose one of the stories you have heard reported.

Imagine you have a story-teller with a unique way of relating the story and think about what kind of language/dialect/colloquialisms/rhythm/imagery the storyteller might use.

6. Write the storyteller's version of the story.
7. Read and discuss.

## The Personal and the Political

Aim: To discover ways of transforming personal experience into political experience.

Method:
1. Discussion about where the personal and the political overlap; e.g. 'a woman's right to choose/the pay gap/no religious attire in certain professions'. Describe the issue with three adjectives.

2. Which writers are successful at blending or juxtaposing the personal and the political; e.g. Alice Walker, Caryl Churchill, Margaret Atwood. Read and discuss passages/instances?

3. Think about the power structure within your own family. Imagine it to be the power structure of a State. Leader may need to discuss these ideas further and give examples.

4. Volunteers each present a tableau, using members of the group to represent the power structure/hierarchy of the imaginary State. Members will present slightly different tableaux; e.g. a colony, a matriarchy, a dictatorship, a country in the grip of civil war. Discuss each tableau and find a word to describe the kind of State depicted, and define the ways in which power is distributed within it.

5. Look at Caryl Churchill's play *Cloud Nine*, Pinter's *Mountain Language* or another substitute text. Read and discuss a part of one of these texts. What kind of power structure does the piece suggest in terms of:
a) the State? (b) the Family?

6. Write your own piece, where the personal and political are intertwined.

7. Share and discuss.

WRITING WORKSHOPS

## Resolutions

**Aim:** To examine how an ending fulfils emotional needs in an audience and resolves the major conflicts of the story.

**Method:**
1. Think of a good and a bad ending to a play, film or novel.

Examples might be plays such as *Top Girls, Waiting for Godot, A Raisin in the Sun* or films such as *The Favourite, Thelma and Louise* or *Parasite*, might be discussed.

2. Compile a list of criteria for good endings.

Did the ending demonstrate the central idea of the play/film? Was it ambiguous or ironic perhaps?

3. In pairs, choose a central idea for a play/film/novel by remembering a time when your ideas or attitude about a person or an issue suddenly changed.

Tell your partner what event made you change your mind in this way.

Swap.

4. Write an account of your partner's story.

5. Take turns reading this back to your partner.

6. Write a piece from an opposite perspective to the one you now hold, that will argue with the account that your partner has drawn.

7. Share this counter-view with your partner in turn.

8. Using two different accounts and opposing views that you and your partner have created, write the scene in which these two opponents confront each other and fight it out to the finish. You have written the final scene of a play.

9. Share and discuss these in the whole group. Can we guess what the central idea is and what the counter idea is? Is the scene successful in resolving the conflict? Does it leave us feeling we want to know more?

10. How was the conflict resolved? Is there a winner and a loser? Discuss.

> "There's enough brackets put on us already. We don't need to bracket our creativity any more than we do."
> – Kae Tempest

# RESOURCE DIRECTORY

## compiled by Saskia Calliste

This resource directory offers a useful list of grants, organisations and publications, in and around the literary world. Many of these organisations are set up to aid the progression of women, and underrepresented groups in the industry, throughout the UK and abroad.

**Grants, Awards and Bursaries (UK)**
Arts Council Awards  artscouncil.org.uk/funding-finder/grants-arts
The Arvon 5-Day Poetry Challenge Competition  arvon.org/5-day-poetry-challenge-thankyou/
Authors' Club Annual Literary Awards  authorsclub.co.uk/
The Bridport Prize  bridportprize.org.uk/
Bruntwood Prize For Playwriting  writeaplay.co.uk/
Commonwealth Writers' Prize  commonwealthwriters.org/
Channel 4 Playwright Scheme  careers.channel4.com/4talent/industry-talent-schemes/channel-4-playwrights-scheme
Costa Book Awards  costa.co.uk/behind-the-beans/costa-book-awards/
Fawcett Society Book Prize/Funny Women Awards  funnywomenawards.com/
H.E. Bates Short Story Competition  hebatescompetition.org.uk/
International Radio Playwriting Competition  bbc.co.uk/writersroom/opportunities/international-radio-playwriting-competition
Life Writing Prize  spreadtheword.org.uk/projects/life-writing-prize/
Live Canon International Poetry Competition  livecanon.co.uk/poetry-competition
London Short Story Prize  spreadtheword.org.uk/projects/london-short-story-prize/

## THE WOMEN WRITERS' HANDBOOK

Northern Writers' Awards  newwritingnorth.com/projects/northern-writers-awards/
Novel Fair  irishwriterscentre.ie/products/submit-to-novel-fair-2020
The Oxford Samuel Beckett Theatre Trust Award  barbican.org.uk/our-story/our-programme/theatre-dance/the-oxford-samuel-beckett-theatre-trust-award
The Poetry Society: National Poetry Competition  poetrysociety.org.uk/competitions/national-poetry-competition/
The Rose Mary Crawshay Prize  thebritishacademy.ac.uk/prizes-medals/rosemary-crawshay-prize
The Royal Literary Fund  rlf.org.uk/
Ryman's Comedy Women in Print Prize  ryman.co.uk/comedywomeninprint
The Society of Authors Awards  societyofauthors.org/Prizes/Society-of-Authors-Awards
Student Playwriting Competition  questors.org.uk/
Verity Bargate Award  sohotheatre.com/artists/writers/verity-bargate-award/
YA Book Prize (Hay Festival)  hayfestival.com/p-15159-the-bookseller-ya-book-prize.aspx
Yorkshire Museum Trust  yorkmuseumstrust.org.uk/
Young Writer Awards (The *Sunday Times*)  youngwriteraward.com/

### Literary Festivals (UK)

*For a full list of literary festivals in the UK:* literaryfestivals.co.uk/
Black Girl Fest  blackgirlfest.com/
Cheltenham Literature Festival  cheltenhamfestivals.com/literature/
Chorlton Women Writers  chorltonbookfestival.co.uk/
Diva Literary Festival  divaliteraryfestival.com/
Dulwich Literary Festival  dulwichliteraryfestival.co.uk
Edinburgh International Book Festival  edbookfest.co.uk/
Hay Festival  hayfestival.com/home
Killer Women Festival  killerwomen.org/
London Book Fair  londonbookfair.co.uk/
London Literary Festival  southbankcentre.co.uk
MFest  mfest.org/
Mayfair and St James Literary Festival  mayfairlitfest.com/
North Cornwall Book Festival  ncornbookfest.org/
Oxford Literary Festival  oxfordliteraryfestival.org/
Raworths Harrogate Literary Festival  harrogateinternationalfestivals.com/raworths-literature-festival/
Stratford Literary Festival  stratfordliteraryfestival.co.uk/

# RESOURCE DIRECTORY

Words Weekend wordsweekend.com/
York Literature Festival yorkliteraturefestival.co.uk/

## Publications & Organisations (UK)

Black Ballad blackballad.co.uk/
The Daily Good thegoodtrade.com/the-daily-good
Everywoman (organisation) everywoman.com/
Feminist Review (peer reviewed journal) journals.sagepub.com/home/fer
gal-dem gal-dem.com/
Pink News (publication) pinknews.co.uk/
Refinery 29 refinery29.com/en-us
Tears In The Fence tearsinthefence.com/
Women's Resource Centre (organisation) wrc.org.uk/

## Related Organisations (UK)

Black Girl Festival blackgirlfest.com/
Cambridge Women's Resources Centre cwrc.org.uk/
Feminist Book Fortnight feministbookfortnight.wordpress.com/
The Feminist Library feministlibrary.co.uk/
Lesbian Archive and information centre discovery.nationalarchives.gov.uk/details/c/F126949
The Pankhurst Centre pankhursttrust.org/
Society of Authors societyofauthors.org/
UK Theatre, Covent Garden uktheatre.org/
The Women's Education Project womenseducationproject.org/
Women In Publishing womeninpublishingsummit.com/
The Writers' Guild of Great Britain writersguild.org.uk/
World Forum Disrupt worldforumdisrupt.com/women-in-publishing-london-19/

## Publishing Houses for Women (UK and International)

Aurora Metro Books aurorametro.com
The Feminist Press feministpress.org/
Girls Talk London girlstalklondon.com/
Honno Welsh Women's Press honno.co.uk/
Inanna Press inanna.ca/
Kelsey St Press kelseyst.com/
Linen Press thelinenpress.co.uk/
Modjaji Books modjajibooks.co.za/
Persephone Books persephonebooks.co.uk/

**THE WOMEN WRITERS' HANDBOOK**

Sapphire Press  sapphirebooks.com/
She Writes Press  shewritespress.com/
Spinifex  spinifexpress.com.au/
Virago Press  virago.co.uk/

## Workshops and Training (UK & Ireland)

A Woman's Write  awomanswrite.com/
Abbey Theatre Dublin  abbeytheatre.ie/
The Arvon Foundation  arvon.org/
The Asian Writer  theasianwriter.co.uk/
Association of Women in the Arts  awita.london/
Clean Break  cleanbreak.org.uk/
Crescent Arts Belfast  crescentarts.org/
Finborough Theatre, ETPEP, Experienced theatre practitioners early playwrighting  finboroughtheatre.co.uk/productions/2019/etpep.php
Glasgow Feminist Writers' Group  glasgowfeministwriters@gmail.com
Glasgow Women's Library  womenslibrary.org.uk/
Irish Women's Network  womensirishnetwork.com/
Killer Women  killerwomen.org/
Liverpool Fringe  liverpoolfringe.co.uk/
The Magdalena Project  themagdalenaproject.org/
The Mandy Network  mandy.com/
Merseyside LGBT Creative Writing Group  liverpoolqueercollective.co.uk/queer-calendar/2018/12/31/merseyside-lgbt-creative-writing-group
New Writing North  newwritingnorth.com/
Old Museum Building  ulsterarchitecturalheritage.org.uk/
Paines' Plough: The Writers' Company  painesplough.com/
Playwrights Studio Scotland  playwrightsstudio.co.uk/
Poetry London  poetrylondon.co.uk/
Second Wave Youth Arts  secondwave.org.uk/
Seven Bridge Writers' Collaborative  sevenbridge.org/
Society of Women Writers and Journalists (SWWJ)  swwj.co.uk/
Soho Theatre  sohotheatre.com/
Sphinx Theatre  sphinxtheatre.co.uk/
Spotlight  spotlight.com/
Superbia  superbia.org.uk/
The Wapping Project  thewappingproject.org/
Women's History Network  womenshistorynetwork.org/
Words of Women  wordsofwomen.com/

# RESOURCE DIRECTORY

WOW (Women On Writing) wow-womenonwriting.com/
WOW (Writing on the Wall) writingonthewall.org.uk/
Write Club writeclub.org.uk/
The Writers and Artists Yearbook writersandartists.co.uk/

## Film Festivals for Women (UK and International)

*For a full list of film festivals internationally:* filmfreeway.com
Bentonville, Arkansas U.S. bentonvillefilm.org/
Birds Eye View birds-eye-view.co.uk/
Black Laurel Films U.S. blacklaurelfilms.com/
Boston Women's Film Festival U.S. bostonwomensfest.org/
Broad Humour U.S. broadhumor.com/
Cairo International Film Festival, Egypt cairowomenfilmfest.com/
Elles Tournent, Belgium ellestournent-damesdraaien.org/
Female Eye Film Festival Canada femaleeyefilmfestival.com/
Femcine, Chile femcine.cl/
Filmdefemmes, France filmsdefemmes.com/
Ifema, Sweden femalefilmfestival.se/
International Film Festival Assen, Netherlands filmfestivalassen.nl/
LaFemme Fest, Los Angeles U.S. lafemme.org/
Films Des Femmes France filmsdefemmes.com/
London Feminist Film Festival londonfeministfilmfestival.com/
London Lesbian Film Festival Canada llff.ca/
Luna Fest U.S. lunafest.org/
Mujeres en Foco, Argentina mujeresenfoco.com.ar/
Nevada Women's Film Festival U.S. nwffest.com/
Reel Sisters of Diaspora Film Festival U.S. reelsisters.com/
Rocky Mountain Women's Film Festival U.S. rmwfilm.org/
St Johns International Women's Festival Canada womensfilmfestival.com/
Underwire underwirefestival.com/
Vancouver Women's Film Festival, Canada womeninfilm.ca/
Women's Comedy Film Festival womenscomedyfilmfestival.com/
Women's international film and arts Festival U.S. womensfilmfest.com/
Women Over Fifty Film Festival wofff.co.uk/

# QUIZ

Can you spot the woman writer? On the front and back covers there are 30 influential, contemporary and historical women writers featured. Can you match the names to the faces?

| | |
|---|---|
| **Chimamanda Ngozi Adichie** | Nawal El Saadawi |
| **Louisa May Alcott** | Anne Frank |
| **Isabel Allende** | Cornelia Funke |
| **Rajaa Alsanea** | Zora Neale Hurston |
| **Maya Angelou** | Harper Lee |
| **Margaret Atwood** | Ursula LeGuin |
| **Jane Austen** | Doris Lessing |
| **Aphra Behn** | Toni Morrison |
| **Malorie Blackman** | J.K. Rowling |
| **Enid Blyton** | Arundhati Roy |
| **Charlotte Bronte** | Sappho |
| **Agatha Christie** | Mary Shelley |
| **Colette** | Harriet Beecher Stowe |
| **Emily Dickinson** | Amy Tan |
| **George Eliot** | Virginia Woolf |

For more great books by women go to:
www.aurorametro.com
For more intelligent non-fiction:
www.supernovabooks.co.uk
follow us on facebook/AuroraMetro
twitter: @aurorametro